Finding God in Strange Places

Gwendolyn Keyes Baker

Copyright © 2019 by Gwendolyn Keyes Baker

All rights reserved. This book or any portion thereof may not be reproduced or used in any manner whatsoever without the express written permission of the publisher except for the use of brief quotations in a book review.

Printed in the United States of America

First Printing, 2019

ISBN 978-1-7333863-1-9 (paperback)

ISBN 978-1-7333863-3-3 (e-book)

MD Publications
www.gwendolynkbaker.com

Dedication

First and foremost, I am so grateful to God for bringing the vision He planted in my spirit many years ago to pass. This book is a brief testimony of the many times God ministered to me amid circumstances I thought would literally take me out. Instead, His grace ushered me into a wealthy place. May He get the glory He so deserves.

I am so blessed that God allowed me to give birth to two beautiful gifts – Kristen Dionne, my firstborn and Kimberly Nyemade, my baby. You have been my inspiration in tough times, and it is to you that I dedicate this book. I am so very amazed at the strong young women you have become. Your boldness, tenacity, kind yet fierce hearts, and passion blesses me.

Thank you for believing in me and encouraging me to hold on in my strange places. You are each such an incredible blessing and I love you more than my vocabulary can convey. I know that God has even greater blessings in store, and I look forward to the fulfillment of all that He has purposed for your lives.

Acknowledgements

To my mom, Alethia, who always told me that I was "*Anna's grand*" and I could accomplish anything I set my mind to. Thank you for your wonderful example of a strong woman with strong faith. I saw you endure difficult times with grace and dignity, and I pray that I will one day become half the woman you are. Thank you so much for your love and support throughout my life.

To my dad, Walter, Jr., who is unconditional love personified. Thank you, daddy, for your words of wisdom that would find its way into our simple times of sharing. Thank you for the many times you told me I was smart – even when I did not feel that I was. Thank you for all the laughs we've had together. They so often did my soul good like medicine. You are certainly the biggest tease.

To my siblings, I am so thankful for each of you and what you each mean to me. I would write something about you individually, but since there are so many of you – please allow this to suffice. You have momma and daddy to thank for that - LOL! Life with you is *'like a box of chocolates'* – there's no telling what we'll get when we're all together. Some are nutty, and others are full of gooey fillings that can come gushing out when pressed. There are a few dark chocolates in the mix, and a sweet delight or two to simply be enjoyed. You figure out where you fall! All jokes aside, I must admit that life wouldn't be the same without you, including our beloved deceased brother, Carlton. Family is everything to me and I'm eternally grateful that you're a part of it.

To Pastor Derrick W. Hutchins, II, thank you for declaring over my life that God said it was time to write. You provided confirmation without even knowing that I had begun the process and I'm so appreciative. It's a blessing to be in God's timing. Much love and respect to you.

To the most amazing writing coach/editor, Tamika Sims, I so appreciate you. You pushed me to give my best and you held me accountable. Thank you so much for helping me to birth this project.

To Dr. Yasha Jones Becton, one whom I greatly respect and admire, thank you so much for introducing the book to readers through the writing of the foreword. Thank you for being true to who you are and obeying God in the directions you spoke to me.

To Kristen, my firstborn. I knew from the day you were born that you were someone special in God. There is no one more appropriate to have written the afterword. Thank you for being who you are and for adding your flavor to the project. I love you in a way no words can explain.

To each beta reader, thank you so much for investing your time to provide feedback and help ensure the message was on target. I appreciate you immensely.

Foreword

We are living in an exciting time. God is advancing His Kingdom and new authors are being catapulted into the marketplace. These authors are immediately broadening and increasing the availability of information and revelation for the modern-day believer. But, while a growing number of new authors are being introduced in this season, new to authorship does not necessarily equate to one being a novice to teaching or preaching the Word of God.

I can still recall a message that Gwendolyn Baker delivered at our local church more than 25 years ago. The message was entitled *"Developed in the Darkroom,"* and it provided a thorough description of how the enemy engages in an intense attack against the untapped potential of future warriors in Christ – much like a skilled bowler forcefully targets the 'kingpin' to achieve a strike in bowling. If he 'strikes' it just right, all the pins tumble. That's the goal of the enemy- to leave our lives in shambles. At the time I was a college student, experiencing an unusual amount of spiritual warfare. Her message helped me realize what I was experiencing and as a result, helped me abandon any ideas of fainting or quitting. It encouraged me to remain steadfast in the faith.

As an author, while she does not sugar coat the principles that the Holy Spirit allows her to share in this book, because of her gracefulness the teachings are offered void of offence and easy to digest. It is truth spoken (or written) in love, without any condemnation or pointing of the finger.

From uprooting bitterness to weathering the unnerving transition of divorce, in *Finding God in Strange Places*, she uses her own personal experiences as a platform for gifting to the reader a higher spiritual perspective. The book highlights the strange, as well as the painful places, in which we may sometimes find ourselves. How to successfully navigate the strange place of losing a child through miscarriage. How to rebound from being placed in a strange place relative to your career or profession. There are certain chapters that are sure to serve as an immediate reference point for a current strange place you are encountering.

Ironically, although I'm currently married, the chapter on the strange place of singleness really resonated with me. There are also several essential wisdom nuggets in this chapter for those that are married or in spiritual leadership. Each chapter is filled with wisdom nuggets.

Gwendolyn Baker is the epitome of the scriptural text Psalm 37:37 which tells us to mark the perfect man (women included). She is valuable in the Kingdom of God as she provides a Godly and mature example for other believers to follow.

Through *Finding God in Strange Places*, we have been granted the rewarding opportunity to sit at her feet and glean from the treasures of her heart as she shares the Word of God and her own personal story. Strange places will be uncovered and showcased as potential places for unprecedented spiritual growth. It is my prayer that as your read you are increased even the more as you rediscover God in the strange places of life. Allow God to produce in you a more excellent spirit by showing you a more excellent way.

Yasha Jones Becton

Pastor, Revealing Word Ministries

Table of Contents

Dedication	iii
Acknowledgements	iv
Foreword	vi
Introduction	1
Chapter 1: The Strange Place of Purpose	7
Chapter 2: The Strange Place of Sacrifice and Surrender	15
Chapter 3: The Strange Place of Fear	25
Chapter 4: The Strange Place of Exhaustion	35
Chapter 5: The Strange Place of Bitterness	43
Chapter 6: The Strange Place of Discipline	51
Chapter 7: The Strange Place of Waiting	59
Chapter 8: The Strange Place Conflict and Confrontation	67
Chapter 9: The Strange Place of Singleness	75
Chapter 10: The Strange Place of Peace	87
Bonus: The Strange Place of Repentance	95
Afterword	98
Works Cited and References	99
About the Author	104

Introduction

"Dear friends, don't be surprised at the fiery trials you are going through, as if something strange were happening to you. Instead, be very glad—for these trials make you partners with Christ in his suffering, so that you will have the wonderful joy of seeing his glory when it is revealed to all the world." (1 Peter 4:12-13 NLT)

Unconventional. Unusual. Perplexing. Surprising in a way that is unsettling or hard to understand. Unfamiliar. Strange.

Have you ever found yourself in a *strange* place? A place that made you feel uncomfortable, uneasy and at times downright afraid? A place or situation you never in your wildest dreams anticipated? A place that brought elements of shock, surprise, uncertainty and perhaps even trauma?

They are the places, situations, and circumstances that lead us to ask questions like, "How in the world did I get *here?!*" "How did *this* happen?!" "Lord, *what in the world* are you doing?!" "How will I *ever* get through this?"

Interestingly, there will be times when we find ourselves in *strange* places not because of our own personal choices, but because of those to whom we are connected. Remember Jonah? Everyone on the ship with him was endangered because of *his* disobedience.

> **There will be times when we find ourselves in strange places not because of our own personal choices, but because of those to whom we are connected.**

There will also be times when – like Hagar and Jesus - our *obedience* lands us right smack in the middle of a *strange* place. Hagar did exactly as she was instructed by Sarai. She became intimate with Abram and bore him a son only to be ill-treated at the hands of the very one who instructed her to do it. And Jesus, He obeyed God to the letter only to ultimately give His life on a rugged cross - not for anything He did, but solely for *our* sins.

> **There will also be times when – like Hagar and Jesus - our obedience lands us right smack in the middle of a strange place.**

I'm sure we can all think of personal examples as well as some that have affected our family and friends. We've seen families suffer because one person is an alcoholic or drug abuser. We've seen a spouse and the children suffer because of the other spouse's infidelity. A friend suffers because the friend she confided in shared trusted secrets and now she must deal with the public humiliation that results. *Strange* places.

Despite the conditions we find ourselves in and what we feel in the moment, we ultimately come to realize that God does not make mistakes. Nothing happens to us that He does not allow. As difficult as it might be, we are right where we should be. And, in some strange way we know that we will be all the better for it – *eventually*. Like the psalmist, we must surrender to the will of God and conclude, '*It was good for me to be afflicted so that I might learn your decrees.*' (Psalm 119:71 NIV)

Strange places often represent an invitation from God to commune with Him. He doesn't command us – He simply invites us to converse with Him about every single detail of our lives. Now, to *converse* denotes that there is both talking and listening between at least two people – a conversation. But, if you're anything like me – there are times when

> **Strange places often represent an invitation from God to commune with Him.**

you've traded that amazing privilege for anxiety, confusion, frustration and even lack. The old familiar hymn declares, "O what peace we often forfeit all because we do not carry everything to God in prayer." Let's pause for a moment and be honest. After all, if we are to experience God in our strange places, we must invite Him to get involved in our situations. Is prayer *really* a priority for you? Or, is it hit and miss? You may even have to honestly confess that you often resort to everything, *but* prayer.

Like any other invitation, God's invitation requires a response. He wants to know our intent – our willingness. He wants our presence and undivided attention. Our surrender. Our listening ear. Our brokenness. He wants it all – and in His Presence we can make the great exchange. Missed some opportunities lately? No worries. He is the God of another chance, and right there *in* our strangest places, we can access His Presence. His Love is unconditional. No matter what we've done or *not* done or where we are, He yet bids us come.

Maybe you're in a quite perplexing place at this very moment. Perhaps you're facing divorce. It could be that you're still single when you really thought you'd be married by now. Or, you're growing old alone with no husband or children to care for you. Perchance you just received an unexpected medical diagnosis or are experiencing a major illness. You might be walking through the untimely death of a loved one or battling with a wayward child. There's even the possibility that you're stunned by an unexpected job loss; or, you're a little frustrated that you aren't where you planned to be in your career by now. You may be in one of the *best* seasons of your life yet somehow still yearning for greater. *Strange* places.

As I examine the course of my life, I can recall countless times I was in a *strange* place. The miscarriage of my first pregnancy. Divorced in my forties after 20 years of marriage with two teenagers to rear. Dealing with the uncertainty associated with having to undergo a biopsy *after* having a follow-up mammogram. Facing a significant pay cut with all the same living expenses. Blessed and so incredibly grateful to have two living parents with long life, but sometimes overwhelmed by the new level of responsibility. *Strange* places.

At one point, I literally saw my life as the accident one witnesses in which the vehicle is so demolished that you know in your heart there can be no sign of life barring a miracle. But, then the victim - barely clinging to life - is transported by medevac to the nearest trauma center where a team of top medical professionals immediately go to work. The waiting family gasps at every sight of a doctor walking their way – terrified that he is coming to announce news they are simply unprepared to hear. Finally, the doctor brings news. Your loved one is alive - *barely*. He provides the horrific details - and declares that the next few hours are critical. If your loved one makes it through this, he will have to learn to walk again, talk again, eat again, to recall again – to perform all the basic functions of life - *again*.

Like me, have you ever had a collision on the highway of life that left you maimed or barely hanging on for life? Or, maybe life has been pretty good for you, but now you're at a crossroad, a place of decision that is essential for going to the next level. Wherever you are on life's continuum, as you read through this book, you'll see that you're not alone. Just as He did for me, God wants to meet you right there in your *strange* place. No, He was never lost, but sometimes we must be reminded that He is ever-present despite our situation.

So, where are you? Take a moment to be honest with God and yourself about where you are at this very moment. Are you in a *strange* place? How did you get there? Great questions, but most important is your response to the question Jesus asked the lame man in John 5:6 NLT, *"Would you like to be whole?"*

No, the question is *not* rhetorical. As we take this journey, you will find opportunities for practical application. Opportunities to stop, ponder, pray and spend quiet time in God's Presence so He can provide the direction you need and/or accomplish the healing work required for your success. So, let's begin.

Practical Application:

Write a brief paragraph honestly stating where you are right now. Then, write a brief prayer to God - pouring out your heart as you begin this journey. I pray that you will experience the Father in a unique and very personal way as we spend this time together.

_____
_____
_____
_____
_____
_____
_____
_____
_____
_____
_____
_____
_____
_____

Chapter 1

The Strange Place of Purpose

"I knew you before I formed you in your mother's womb. Before you were born, I set you apart and appointed you...." (Jeremiah 1:5a NLT)

Perhaps nothing has plagued and confounded mankind more than the age-old questions of *'Why am I here?'* and *'What is my purpose?'* So, let's briefly delve into the concept of *purpose*. So often purpose is treated as something mysterious, secretive and out of our reach. But the scripture tells us in Jeremiah 29:11 NLT that God, *"Knows the plans He has for us. They are plans for good and not for disaster, to give us a future and a hope."* The Lord goes on to tell us in verses 12-13, *"When you pray, I will listen. If you look for me wholeheartedly, you will find me."* Very simply put, we are all called to the primary purpose of worshiping God. However, God has a specific plan or purpose for each of our lives that we will come to know as we pray and seek Him with our whole hearts. Though purpose often feels evasive, God has not hidden it from us. He simply reveals it as we wholeheartedly pursue Him. It's like reading the

> **Perhaps nothing has plagued and confounded mankind more than the age-old questions of 'Why am I here?' and 'What is my purpose?'**

instructions that come with a purchase. They will reveal the item's purpose, how it is to be assembled and how it works.

If we're honest, however, most of us will have to admit that our search for purpose – at least initially - did not include seeking God through prayer and the Word. It's easier to pursue what we *think* we should be doing – just like trying to assemble the bike, furniture or other purchase without reading the instructions. I can clearly remember my daughter, who is a millennial, telling me, *"Mom, we don't read instructions."* That is exactly how most of us approach purpose. We don't read the Bible, our Instruction Manual. But the mystery is will be removed and we will experience the simplicity of walking out our purpose when we spend time with God daily, listen to His voice and follow His instructions. Proverbs 16:9 NLT tells us, *"We can make our plans, but the Lord determines our steps."* Do you really want to know, understand and live your purpose? Commit now to pursuing God in prayer. Sounds too simple doesn't it? It's simple but make no mistake, it is *not* easy. Why? Because there is a real enemy that does not want us to realize our purpose, or commit to living it out once we know, and we must be prepared for that daily battle.

Before I go further, let me acknowledge those of you reading this and thinking, I am *crystal* clear about my purpose and confident about what I'm called to do. That's awesome and I applaud you. How exciting to experience the glory; to walk in a greater degree of obedience; to take on more of His character and accomplish the 'greater works' He decreed in John 14: 12. But, I also know that just as seasons change in the natural, we experience them in the spiritual. II Corinthians 3:18 NLT tells us, *"So all of us who have had that veil removed can see and reflect the glory of the Lord. And the Lord—who is the Spirit—makes us more and more like him as we are changed into his glorious image."* God never leaves us where we are. We go from glory to glory, and each level brings along an element of *strange*. How are you being transformed more and more into His Image, so He can accomplish even greater through you? That's a requirement for each of us no matter where we are on our journey.

Now, I am not ashamed to tell you that I've struggled with purpose. Growing up, I was *different*. I am the fourth of eight children and perhaps the only introvert. I was rather shy, tall, lanky – and very knock-kneed. Imagine those traits in elementary school! I can still rather vividly remember being called *grasshopper* and *daddy long legs*. I am also built quite differently than my sisters and, admittedly, I struggled with it for a very long time. My temperament is even different.

In all honesty, as an adult I've asked God what is up with my uniqueness and why I got all the *strange* characteristics. I'll never forget the day Isaiah 45:9 slapped me in the face during one of my rants. It reads, "*Woe to him who strives with him who formed him, a pot among earthen pots. Does the clay say to him who forms it, what are you making? Your work has no handles.*" In other words, how are you, the *created*, going to tell me, the *Creator*, how to make you? In the text, God used Cyrus, a man who neither knew nor honored Him as God, to accomplish His will. Israel was not happy just as you and I are sometimes unhappy about God's choices. However, He can choose and use whomever He will – flaws and all. How dare we question His ability and right to do so?

I know *now* that I am not alone. Like many of you reading these pages, I was caught up in the comparison trap. I believed the lies that played over and over in my head, and that ultimately led to my feelings of insecurity. Those lies shook my confidence early in life. As Satan often does, he perverted the very things God deposited into my life for His purpose and glory. Comparison is a tactic of the enemy of which we must not be ignorant. When we compare ourselves to others, we will likely try to emulate them instead of being the authentic, unique individuals we were created to be. At best, we will become fakes when God created, gifted, graced and anointed us for the race He set before *us*.

When we focus on what He gave to others, we become distracted from the joy and fulfillment intended for us. Comparison essentially tells us we will never be good enough, and if we are not careful, we will exhaust ourselves trying to become what we were never even designed to be. No matter what we accomplish or how well it's done, comparison will leave us feeling unfulfilled. It's a trap we've all experienced at some point – some perhaps in larger doses than others. I did. But, despite the circumstances and my feelings, I still had the audacity to dream!

> **When we focus on what He gave to others, we become distracted from the joy and fulfillment intended for us.**

Since I was very young, I dreamed of a bright future with great accomplishments. Even though I grew up in a family with parents who did not complete high school and no one in my immediate family who had attended college, I clung to the dream of going to and graduating college. Of earning my degree and becoming a family counselor.

Do you dream about accomplishing things that no one in your family - or even among your friends – has ever attempted, yet alone accomplished? It's because God created you with *purpose*. At the same time, the enemy of our soul peeps the cards to our future and sets in motion his plan to steer us away from our God-given purpose.

Just like the prophet Jeremiah in Jeremiah 1:5, God knew us and ordained our purpose before we were even formed in our mother's womb. It must become our life's mission to learn and pursue our purpose. So, what's the challenge? Often the purpose and plan of God represents a *strange* place for many of us. It's sometimes totally different from what we have envisioned for ourselves. Or, we don't see ourselves as worthy or capable of the assignment. In some cases, we clearly understand the call; however, the weight and requirements it carries *terrifies* us. We don't want to make the sacrifice it demands of us or we want to be *normal* – like everyone else - so we run from the mantle. Like Jeremiah, Moses and Gideon, we give God a laundry list of reasons why we are *not* the one for the job. As a result, we spend years trying to escape the very thing that will bring us the greatest fulfillment and the success we seek.

Have you been running away from your God-ordained purpose? Or, from the elevation God is trying to bring you into? From a specific assignment? The Bible tells us in Jonah 1:3a NLT, *"Jonah got up and went in the opposite direction to get away from the Lord.* What have you pursued in lieu of purpose? Where has your disobedience landed you? Jonah 1:4 NLT tells us, *"But the Lord hurled a powerful wind over the sea, causing a violent storm that threatened to break the ship apart."* Like Jonah, are you in the belly of unique circumstances or a storm that God prepared *just* for you? A storm that threatens to break your very life apart? A *strange* place? You're not alone. I've been there.

Some of the places I landed were horrible and seemingly hopeless. But, just as God promised in His Word, He was right there with me. The Psalmist declared in Psalms 139:8 KJV, *"If I ascend up into heaven, thou art there; if I make my bed in hell, behold, thou art there."* He never left me nor did He forsake me, even though it sometimes felt like I could not find Him anywhere. Even though I could not sense His Presence, He came through for me in ways unimaginable!

I have learned that I will not experience true fulfillment until I embrace God's purpose for my life. That requires me to seek Him daily for direction, attune my ears to hear His voice and obediently follow Him in complete surrender. The *strange* place of purpose necessitates a daily *yes* which means I must often pray Philippians 2:13 NLT, *"God, please work in me, and give me the desire and power to do what pleases you."* Do I always succeed? No. But I'm thankful for His grace and mercy that allows me to start fresh daily.

As I'm walking through life's challenges, I'm getting to know God in a more intimate way. The more I seek Him the more I see how flawed I am, and how much I need Him. I also see how much He loves me despite me and I am simply humbled. It is these times that are building my character and preparing me for my purpose – especially during this season in which I am called to pour into women the wisdom God is birthing in me. It is the preparation God knew I'd need for my assignment.

So, let's talk seasons for a moment. A season is defined as a period characterized by a circumstance or feature. In the natural, the various seasons can bring about a significant change in the weather and the environment. As a result, we dress differently, our behavior and activities change, and sometimes our health is even impacted – all because of the season.

Our lives also have seasons. Ecclesiastes 3:1 NLT tells us, 'For everything there is a season, a time for every activity under heaven. There is a season of transition, of suffering, of silence, of stillness, of conflict, of waiting (the one we all probably dislike most!), a season of singleness of marriage and parenting, – to name just a few. Life and priorities are different in each of these seasons – and sometimes we're in more than one at the *same* time. I've been in a season of transition on many levels. I'm aging, have had a career change and I'm experiencing the changing needs of my parents. At the same time, I am also in a season of waiting. There are some unfulfilled promises I'd like to have now that have not yet manifested. Whew, what a journey!

I'm comforted, though, in knowing seasons change. While it is not easy, it has helped me to embrace each one – trusting that God will fulfill the promise of His Word in Psalm 1:2-3. The passage reminds us that we are blessed when we take delight in God's Word and meditate on it day and night. As a result, we will be like trees planted by the river - bearing forth fruit in each season and prospering in all we do. Joseph is a prime example of this. He was sold by his brothers, falsely accused by Potiphar's wife, sent to prison – and despite all that, the Bible declares more than one time, '*The*

Lord was with him and caused everything he did to prosper.' (Genesis 39:23b)

What season are you in? Do you know God's purpose for *that* season? Have you fully embraced it? For those of you who have, how are you growing and being transformed on a continual basis? I recently happened upon a sermon Dr. Myles Munroe preached in 2017 the year before he passed. He spoke extensively concerning purpose and how he sought God early in his life regarding purpose. He made this point – which I don't think I will ever forget. He said that, 'God is committed to our success because His reputation is on the line.' He went on to say that nugget gave Him a boldness to pursue great things from God and we all know his powerful legacy lives on years beyond his demise. God is equally committed to your success – and mine – so let's pursue Him boldly.

> **God is committed to our success because His reputation is on the line.'**

Practical Application

What has God called and purposed you to do? What are you passionate about? Briefly write out your purpose statement below.

_____
_____
_____
_____
_____

Don't know or haven't fully embraced your purpose, spend some time quietly listening for His response and write down what you hear.

_____
_____
_____
_____
_____

Write a brief prayer to God about what you wrote and about walking in your God-ordained purpose.

_____
_____
_____
_____
_____

Chapter 2

The Strange Place of Sacrifice and Surrender

"And so, dear brothers and sisters, I plead with you to give your bodies to God because of all he has done for you. Let them be a living and holy sacrifice--the kind he will find acceptable. This is truly the way to worship him. Don't copy the behavior and customs of this world, but let God transform you into a new person by changing the way you think. Then you will learn to know God's will for you, which is good and pleasing and perfect." Romans 12:1-2 NLT

In our previous lesson we took a deep dive into understanding purpose. Now that we have laid the foundation, let's talk about the strange place of sacrifice and surrender. Why? Because once we know and understand our purpose, a new battle begins!

The first 11 chapters of Romans details the doctrine of salvation and all that God did for us. In chapter 12, it turns practical and focuses on what we are to do in response. The Apostle Paul does not command us, but with a heart of compassion – encourages us by the *'mercies of God'* to present our bodies as a living sacrifice to God.

I have always been intrigued by the phrase *living sacrifice*. Throughout the Old Testament, animal sacrifices were killed and placed on the altar as the atonement, or payment, for sin. They represented a foreshadowing of Jesus Christ, the sacrificial Lamb of God. However, because of Christ's ultimate, once-for-all death on the cross, the Old Testament system of offering a dead sacrifice was dismissed (Hebrews 9:11-12).

Remember the story of Abraham and Isaac? God instructed Abraham to offer Isaac, his only son whom he and Sarah had in their old age, as a sacrifice. Really God? You want what he loved so dearly and waited on for so long? Yes. Sacrifice *costs*. David acknowledged this in II Samuel 24:24, when he declared "*I will not present burnt offerings to the Lord my God that have cost me nothing.*"

> **Sacrifice costs.**

Despite the cost of the sacrifice Abraham moved in obedience, trusting that God would provide a way out. He took Isaac to the mountain, bound and laid him on the altar. As he raised his hand to slay him, God stopped him and proclaimed, '*now I know.*' What of great importance has God asked you to sacrifice? How did you respond? Can God say, '*now I know?*'

In the New Testament, the call to offer oneself as a *living* sacrifice is now our essential or supreme act of worship. We who are Christ's through our saving faith in Him are instructed to offer, or present, ourselves completely to God. Given Jesus' ultimate sacrifice, this is only reasonable. But, it's not easy!

In the Old Testament, because the animal was dead when offered on the altar, it could only be *presented* to the Lord once as a sacrificial offering. In the New Testament, *we* are urged to present ourselves to God as a *living* sacrifice, which implies that we must live in a continual state of surrender and consecration. Our commitment may begin with an important, "*once-and-for-all*" decision, but we must see every day of our lives as another day — another opportunity — to surrender and offer our lives as a sacrifice to God.

As living sacrifices, we will feel the pain of the refiner's fire as we lay prostrate on the altar. Yet, we cannot crawl off. We must remain, totally surrendered, so God can transform us into vessels of honor meet for His use. It will require great humility and a total dependence on God, but Jesus is our example of a living sacrifice and the awesome power that comes from totally surrendering to God. He endured the cross despising the shame and is now seated on the right hand of the Father interceding for you and me (Hebrews 12:2b). He is praying for us!

> **As living sacrifices, we will feel the pain of the refiner's fire as we lay prostrate on the altar.**

So, let's talk about what offering oneself as a living sacrifice looks like in practical everyday life. I love watching HGTV and seeing homes transformed from an eyesore to a beautiful living space. It is fascinating to watch, and I see a striking parallel between those transformations and our lives. To conform means to fit the mold or pattern; to do as others do. To transform means to make a thorough or dramatic change in the outward form or appearance of; to change in character or condition; convert. So, it simply means that begin by offering God the sacrifice of a broken spirit and a broken, repentant heart, (Psalm 51: 17 NLT). We are no longer to fit the pattern or mold of the world in which we live, but we are to be dramatically changed in our appearance and character daily by a new mindset (v.2). That means we have offered our souls to God to be saved. In Psalm 116:12 NLT the psalmist asks, *'What can I offer the Lord for all he has done for me?'* The only acceptable answer is in Romans 12:2. We offer ourselves and it begins with offering our soul - the foundation for being a living sacrifice. It is implied in v. 1 with the use of the words, *'dear brothers and sisters.'*

Next, we must present our body as a holy and living sacrifice. Apostle Paul previously admonished us in Romans 6:13 NLT, *'Do not let any part of your body become an instrument of evil to serve sin. Instead, give yourselves completely* to God, for you were dead, but now you have new life. So, use your whole body as an instrument to do what is right for the glory of God.'* This is really the process of sanctification which involves the daily offering of body to God in righteous living. I Thessalonians 4:3-5 NLT says, *'God's will is for you to be holy, so stay away from all sexual sin. Then each of you will control his own body and live in holiness and honor not in lustful passion like the pagans who do not know God and his ways.'* We are commanded to not love the world nor the things it offers us.

Then, we must surrender our mind to God. This is critical because if we don't give God our minds and allow Him to transform it, we will not offer our bodies to Him as a living sacrifice. The Bible tells us in Proverbs 23:7a KJV, *'As a man thinketh in his heart, so is he'* so if our minds are not transformed, what we think will ultimately control our bodies. In the words of renowned televangelist Joyce Meyer, *'Where the mind goes, the body will follow.'* The mind must be deprogrammed from the worldly way of thinking. I John 2:14-15 defines three components of the *'world'* – lust of the flesh, lust of the eyes and the pride of life. All the temptations that the world offers us can be reduced to these three things.

The lust of the flesh refers to the temptation to feel physical pleasure from some sinful activity that makes the flesh and our appetites satisfied. It is not only sex, but can also be things like gossiping, food or a gluttonous spirit, drink or any of the other sins outlined in Galatians 5:19-21.

The lust of the eyes is the temptation to look at things we shouldn't or to have things we shouldn't have. Coveting – a yearning or a strong desire for something that rightfully belongs to someone else - is a prime example of the lust of the eyes. It mostly involves coveting what we see that we don't have and envying those who have what we want. One example is to want another person's spouse because of how their relationship *appears*. Other examples include looking at pornography or desiring others' material possessions, status and appearance. A prime example is the story of King David as he looked at Bathsheba and saw that she was 'very beautiful to look upon,' (2 Samuel 11:2). That act led to other sins – including murder.

The pride of life is defined by any ambition for that which puffs us up and puts us on the *throne* of our own lives. It causes us to desire excess greatness or power. God hates this sin the most as it made Lucifer, the beautiful angel, turn into Satan, the adversary. Examples include desiring/taking credit or glory for things that others or God did; desiring for others to hold us in high esteem or *worship* us; or wanting to feel valued or more important than others around us. We *must* be transformed by renewing our mind with the power of God's Word in order to be the living sacrifice God can accept.

Finally, we must surrender our will so we can prove, or demonstrate, by our lives what the will of God is. In other words, when we as believers do the will of God, we put His will on display for the world to see. Let me go ahead and tell you it is not easy. Our flesh wants nothing to do with the will of God – and that is why we must crucify it daily. We won't love our enemies or do good to those who despitefully use us if we don't surrender our will and, therefore, crucify our flesh. Our constant prayer must be, 'Father, work in me both to will and do of your good pleasure.' It is only by the mercies of God that we can do it.

We live in a self-obsessed, self-absorbed age and as believers, we must be very careful. God wants us to enjoy all the good gifts that come from Him. What He doesn't want is for us to want them more than we want Him. For us to forsake intimacy with Him, the Creator, as we pursue what He has created. He loves us so much, but we often make *idols* out of the things He's created instead of lavishing Him

> **We must stay on the altar daily – and crucify the idols of self, security, success, comfort, approval and everything else we so often put on His throne.**

with our love and receiving His blessings as a result. After all, He promised that He would not withhold any good thing from those who love Him. That's why we must stay on the altar daily – and crucify the idols of self, security, success, comfort, approval and everything else we so often put on the throne that should belong only to Him.

How are you doing with *offering* yourself as a living sacrifice? What is God asking you to give up in the process that is near and dear to your heart – that you are struggling to release? Your time? Money? An unhealthy relationship? Forgiveness to someone you don't think deserves it? To love someone who had hurt you deeply? Is He asking you to simply relinquish control of a situation that has you wringing your hands because you have no idea how to fix it? Is He asking you to simply be still and know Him as God? One of our greatest struggles is to rest in God and let Him handle the things we're dealing with. It requires us to surrender control and trust the all-knowing, all-powerful, ever-present God with every detail of our lives.

As I was walking through my divorce years ago, there were many details I had to handle. Some things I faced were extremely difficult and I really didn't know what to do or *frankly* even how to feel. It's an emotional enough experience to deal with the hurt of divorce, but then to add the decisions about what to do with the home, the children, joint assets and everything else is quite overwhelming. We had to make a decision about the home and we couldn't seem to agree. My bank account said I could not keep it, and it also said I couldn't afford to find something else – at least not that I was comfortable with for me and my daughters. I learned what the expression, '*running around like a chicken with no head*' means. I was frantic at first! But at every turn, however, Psalm 46:10, '*Be still and know that I am God…*' slapped me upside the head. I was so sick and tired of that scripture! I didn't want to be still, I wanted God to fix it – *now*. Surprise! He didn't. And I struggled. And became depressed and despondent, and drifted in my relationship with Him. But nothing changed until I learned to be still – to get off the *throne*, His rightful place, and onto the *altar* where I belonged.

Then one day, it happened. I was talking with a gentleman about some investments (why? I'm not sure because I had no money! I still had dreams though) and he gave me a piece of advice. He encouraged me to go back to my husband and ask him to just give me the house. I didn't know this man and he didn't know me, but I sensed the still, small voice of God in his instructions. While I was nervous and a bit hesitant to act on it, I did. All he said was, *'I'd already decided to give it to you as is. You take care of anything that needs to happen with it.'* God had intervened and I walked into it with ease and grace. Over time, God provided everything I needed for the home – for repairs, the mortgage (I never missed one payment!), and when I sold it four years ago now, we had a contract in three days – before the for sale sign even went up. God is faithful!

To surrender is to give oneself up into the power of another. To yield to the power, control or possession of another, upon compulsion or demand. To stop fighting, hiding, resisting; to give the control or use of oneself to someone else (God); to completely give up our own will and subject our thoughts, ideas and deeds to the will and teachings of Jesus Christ.

Surrender is not our *natural* inclination – not even for the believer. We meditate on the problem – mulling it over, trying to figure it out. Simply put - we doubt God. I Peter 5:7 NLT tells us, *'Give all your worries and cares to God, for He cares about you.'* Philippians 4:6 NLT, tell us, *'Don't worry about anything; instead, pray about everything. Tell God what you need and thank Him for all He has done.'* But we go kicking and screaming because it goes against the grain. Personally, I had to acknowledge that my fear and lack of trust was the result of my experience with man – which I ultimately projected onto God. It wasn't intentional, but it was uncomfortable to entrust my life into someone else's hand – even though it was God. It requires great discipline daily and a transformation in my thought life.

In studying, I learned that surrender is a battle or military term that implies giving up all rights to the conqueror. It is most appropriate since we are in a spiritual battle *daily*. It begins the day we accept Jesus Christ as Savior and continues daily – moment-by-moment until the day we leave this earth.

There are also different levels of surrender – from the initial submission to the Holy Spirit's drawing to times of greater surrender that brings deeper intimacy with God and greater power in service. The more we surrender to God, the more the Holy Spirit can fill us with His Presence. The more we surrender to God, the more our self-serving, self-worshiping nature dies and is replaced with the Spirit of God. II Corinthians 5:17 declares, *"If any man be in Christ He is a new creature. Old things are passed away and behold, all things have become new."*

We will not experience God in His Fullness until we are truly disciplined to offer ourselves daily as living sacrifices. Galatians 2:20 declares, *"I have been crucified with Christ, and it is no longer I who live, but Christ lives in me. So the life I now live in the body, I live because of the faithfulness of the Son of God, who loved me and gave himself for me.* It's an uncomfortable or *strange* place -but if we walk it out, it will lead us to a place of great power and victory. The words of the hymn, *Is Your All on the Altar* sums it up beautifully –'You have longed for sweet peace, and for faith to increase, you have earnestly, fervently prayed; but you cannot have rest, or be perfectly blessed until all on the altar is laid. The chorus says, 'Is your all on the altar of sacrifice laid? Your heart does the spirit control? You can only be blessed and have peace and sweet rest, as you yield Him your body and soul.' Now, that's the life of a *living* sacrifice.

Practical Application

What is an area where you are not fully yielded to God as a living sacrifice?

_____
_____
_____
_____
_____
_____
_____

What is God asking you to surrender or sacrifice?

_____
_____
_____
_____
_____
_____
_____

Using the Word of God, write a brief prayer to God about where you are and ask for His help to surrender. Remember, He can handle your truth.

_____
_____
_____
_____
_____
_____
_____

Chapter 3

The Strange Place of Fear

'For God has not given us a spirit of fear and timidity, but of power, love, and self-discipline.' (II Timothy 1:7 NLT)

Another suspicious package containing explosive devices sent. Two sisters missing since August found dead. One person killed during a home invasion. These are three news headlines to my phone within the last few hours. I literally had to change the settings to stop the notifications.

With so much happening in our world today, it is so easy – even as believers if we're not careful – to become overly anxious and fearful. As I read the headlines and thought of my family – daughters, nieces and nephews, aging parents – I could feel the fear and anxiety creeping into my heart as I laid in bed at home *alone*.

> **The decision to open my Bible was an invitation for God to meet me right where I was.**

But as is often the case, the Word of God in my devotional was right on time. It was a reminder to me that God is our ever-present help amidst whatever situation we may find ourselves. My decision to open my Bible was an invitation for Him to meet me right where I was.

What is fear? According to Merriam-Webster, fear is *an unpleasant emotion – whether real or perceived - caused by the belief that someone or something is dangerous, likely to cause pain, or a threat.* In the verb form, it is *to be afraid of (someone or something) as likely to be dangerous, painful, or threatening.* While we often think negatively about fear, it is important to understand that fear is natural and serves to warn us of the presence or anticipation of danger – with the goal of helping us avoid the danger. It is likely to be the initial response of each of us.

The Bible, however, talks about two types of fear. The first kind of fear is the *fear or reverence* of the Lord, which is healthy and to be encouraged. This type of *fear* does not mean being afraid. Instead, it means we reverence and honor our Almighty God, the Creator of all things. The One who loved us so much that He gave His only Son to die for us even while we were deep in our sin and cared nothing about Him. It means we have an attitude of respect and awe for all God is, including His unfailing love, mercy, power, and glory as well as characteristics like His righteous anger and wrath.

The fear of the Lord has many blessings and benefits, and it leads to wisdom and understanding (Psalm 111:10). Also, with the fear of the Lord is life and true rest (Proverbs 14:27; 19:23). It is the kind of fear or reverence most of us would have for our parents. Because of our love and respect for who they are and what they have done for us, we strive to not displease them. The same is true of God. We strive to please Him in all we say and do because we love and appreciate all that He is and all He has done for us. It becomes our mission to be pleasing to Him and to bring honor to His name.

The second kind of fear the Bible talks about is a *"spirit of fear"* (2 Timothy 1:7), which is a hindrance to our life and walk with God. It does not come from God. Fear is a tool that our enemy, the devil, uses to hinder us in any way he can from all that God has for us. It is really a lack of trust in our more than trustworthy God.

We are commanded more than 365 times in scripture to, *'fear not'* or *'do not be afraid.'* That's literally at least one command per day for a year. God really wanted us to get that message, but do you sometimes battle with fear? Honestly, sometimes I do. In fact, 2018 was a year in which I struggled with fear and anxiety in a way I don't recall ever doing before. I've always been a strong woman, but even strong women can struggle with fear and insecurities. After a job reclassification and second pay cut in May, I found myself $41,000 short of the salary on which I had become accustomed to living. Same expenses, same responsibilities and almost half the pay. And in all honesty, it *rocked* my world. I'd downsized and purchased a new home just two years earlier and another vehicle less than a year earlier. My mind was racing with questions about how I'd manage. After all, there was no other income since I am a single lady.

> *We are commanded more than 365 times in scripture to, 'fear not' or 'do not be afraid.'*

After a few months of supplementing the salary with my dwindling savings and part-time income, I began to panic about how I would sustain the situation long-term. I was so focused on the problem, that I wasn't being solution focused. I really couldn't *see* how I would make it and I was extremely anxious. After all, I was almost 60. It made sense that I would be *concerned*. I wanted to be responsible and take care of my bills in a timely manner the way I should. But my response was more than concern.

In this life, we will face things that cause our initial or blink reaction to be fear. But, when we are strong and know our God, what we are experiencing will not *paralyze* us. As it does in the natural, paralysis will also cause inaction or a lack of movement, either in part or wholly, in the spiritual. Partial obedience is still disobedience and that is the enemy's goal – to get us to fear to the point that we will not trust and obey God. And you know what, it isn't even about me or you, it's about his vendetta with God. He hates

God and uses us, God's children, to get to Him. Oh, you don't believe me. Job is my witness. The devil went to God and accused Him of protecting Job and insisted that if God would remove the hedge, Job wouldn't serve Him. Job proved him wrong – but what about you and me? Will we prove Him wrong?

The enemy is shrewd and literally went in for the kill. I had to constantly battle thoughts like, '*I feel like the working poor struggling to make ends meet.*' And if that wasn't enough, the enemy began to bombard my mind with feelings of insecurity and inadequacy. I had given my life to a career anticipating that I'd rest easy in my seasoned years, only to find myself questioning how I would make it given the situation. I was literally heartbroken and get this - I felt ashamed as though I had failed. It was certainly a reminder of how quickly life can change. But most importantly, it was a wake-up call to let me see how much I'd come to depend on the job and my ability to earn rather than on God. Because of that dependence, I had to fill the gap – or so I thought. Rather than trusting God, I nearly wore myself out trying to make up the difference.

Now, don't get me wrong, we should do our due diligence to ensure we take care of our responsibilities. I just didn't take the time to truly seek God about what He wanted me to do. Yes, I prayed. Yes, I read the Word. Yes, I listened for His voice during the sermons – and I believed that I'd heard Him on what to do next. Yet, if I'm honest, I was fearful and fear made me doubt what I heard. I ramped up my business activities only to find myself worn out and still lacking what I needed. Where I was accustomed to experiencing success, God allowed me to hit brick walls. I felt like a total failure and I was so exhausted.

As women we are designed to create and give birth. Many of us are creative and can often take what some would toss out and make a beautiful masterpiece. I am often intrigued by what a sister friend does with old furniture. Her home looks like something out of a magazine after she restores old, broken pieces. But sometimes life's challenges can leave us feeling barren, and afraid to create or give birth to the dreams and visions growing inside of us. We can be full of ideas yet so paralyzed by fear, that we are unable to produce – even though we'd done so many times before. I had failed so many times in recent weeks that I was literally afraid to try. I feared failing – *again* – despite all the ideas that were swimming around in my head. Sometimes we can even start the process of *birthing* the vision inside of us then allow fear to cause a *miscarriage*. Fear is detrimental for the believer – and it certainly was for me.

Then one day I happened upon an article titled, "*Three Reasons Why Every Woman Should Embrace Fear.*" I was immediately intrigued by it because we so often think of fear as something to avoid like the plague – even though we *all* experience it. However, fear - *if* handled properly - does have benefits. In the article the author asked, 'When was the last time you *embraced* fear? Even *appreciated* it?" He went on to say, "Most women do everything they can to avoid doing the things that scare them most. Fear, after all, is a very uncomfortable thing." My takeaway message is that feeling fear is really an indication that we are endeavoring to do something big, something that will yield incredible results once we're on the other side of it – if we push through the fear.

Now, let's examine the author's three key reasons for embracing fear. First, fear creates a decision point. We must simply understand that we, *not fear*, are in control and therefore choose to walk into fear so we can discover what is on the other side of it. Secondly, fear will stretch us further than we *ever* thought we could go. We often get stuck in the rut of safety and security, and it will take a little fear and challenge to shake us up and set us on the path to growth and change. Finally, fear can make us feel *alive*. It triggers a '*fight or flight*' reaction that literally causes changes to our physical bodies. Our adrenaline levels soar, our heartbeat quickens, and our breathing accelerates. We experience a sense of accomplishment when we conquer the fear, and it makes us ready for the next challenge. Faith is not an absence of fear, rather it is the choice to act, to obey *regardless* of the fear. Do you think for one moment that Daniel and his friends didn't feel some fear as they stared into the mouth of the lions? We all know what Israel felt when they were told to possess the land flowing with milk and honey – and giants! The only difference in the two is that Daniel and others trusted God despite what they felt.

Everyone has or will experience fear in their lives at some point. I'm not alone and neither are you. Sometimes the fear is subtle, so we may not even see it for what it is. It comes under the guise of excuses – not enough time, money, support. The truth is – *fear* is really the root cause and it's not what God wants for us. To overcome fear, we must trust God completely and receive His unconditional love. I John 4:18 tells us, *"There is no fear in love, but perfect love casts out fear. For fear has to do with punishment, and whoever fears has not been perfected in love."* Satan will do all he can to get us to doubt God's love for us, often by using fear. Fear of the future, what people think of us, failure, you name it—when we believe lies of fear, it gets in the way of experiencing and living out the freedom of God's perfect love.

I've got great news! When we experience fear, (and we all will at some point), we don't have to stay there. Psalm 34:4 declares, *"I sought the LORD, and he answered me and delivered me from all my fears."* This verse reminds us that when we take our fears to God, He hears and He will deliver us. We can't do it on our own. Confessing our fears to God takes the power out of its control over us and allows God

> **Confessing our fears to God takes the power out of its control over us and allows God to cleanse us from it.**

to cleanse us from it, (1 John 1:9). This is simply an active way we can trust God completely. The more we learn to trust Him and His love for us, the more we will experience His peace (Philippians 4:7), and the less fear has any place in our lives. We may still feel the fear initially, so just do it afraid. God will meet you there in that *strange* place.

When I finally just stopped, refocused and poured my heart out to God, He met me right there in my storm. I had difficulty being still and releasing the situation to His control. It is a battle I had to fight in daily small doses – asking, *'God what do you want me to do? You know my situation. I have no one to ask and I don't want to!'* It didn't feel good, but I was right where He wanted me – on the altar for much-needed alterations.

In many ways, I identified with the widow of Zarephath who had just enough to make the last meal for her and her son. In that dire situation, the man of God tells her to serve him first, (I Kings 17). What a test of faith! She could have murmured and complained as many of us would have done, but her faith - which resulted in her obedience - caused a shift in her situation. Yes, our obedience requires *faith*. I can think of numerous times when I'd planned out what I would give based on my carnal view of what I had in my account or at my disposal. But often, the Word would ignite my faith which then triggered me to obey the man of God and trust God with the results.

Of course, there were those times when, like Peter, I took my eyes off Christ and put them onto my situation – causing my faith to waver. In those moments I had to pray like the father in Mark 9:24b NLT, "I do believe, but help me overcome my unbelief." I would read and re-read the passage about the widow to strengthen my faith. I gave sacrificially when I really couldn't *afford* to give. I gave of my time when I could use it to focus on my personal agenda, and of my talent when internally I felt that I had nothing left to give. Sometimes I felt drained, but I'm a living witness that we can never out-give God. Luke 6:38 NLT admonishes us, *'Give and you will receive. Your gift will return to you in full – pressed down, shaken together to make room for more, running over, and poured into your lap. The amount you give will determine the amount you get back.'* While I don't have what I'd like to have *yet*, like the widow of Zarephath, my supply is not exhausted. God provides what I need and more. When I settled myself, and got out God's way, then He opened doors. He connected me with human resources who then helped me with ways to use my financial resources to support me now and in the future. With that need met, I could focus on the dreams and visions in my heart.

For as long as I can remember I've been interested in entrepreneurship. There had been prophesies spoken over me about wealth, but I got comfortable in my jobs because of the *security* I thought they provided. At the same time, I *ached* to pursue the dreams locked up inside, but was afraid to step out. We've been conditioned to stay with what is *sure*; however, I felt such freedom and fulfillment when I was working my businesses. They just weren't generating enough income - *yet*. In all honesty, I really wasn't giving them enough attention for the growth I wanted to see. I did a lot of other things and then had little to no time or energy for the businesses. Had I missed the still small voice of God trying to prepare me for what I'd face? How many ideas had He given me that I started, but didn't finish? That I didn't even *start* because of fear? How many times did I see others give birth to an idea that God had given me that I'd made excuses about why I couldn't do it? My daughters can attest to the fact that a business exists today only miles from the spot where I'd dreamed and talked about putting the *exact* type of business!

Yet right there in that shattered, broken place – in one of my toughest times in life, God met me. I love how He'd speak to my wounded heart as I read His Word or a devotional – or sat in church listening to the sermon. I was learning to pay attention to His whispers and to write down the things I heard. I was *learning* how to be still and know the all-knowing, ever-present God - my good, good Father - who provides. Just as He promised, He provided for my needs – not according to my bank accounts or my efforts. In fact, I began to see Him *direct* resources to me. There were mornings I'd wake up to an order from my website or via text – from customers as well as from referrals whom I'd never even met. While sitting at my kitchen table, I heard an idea that I began to implement is currently generating revenue. Even the very book that you're reading is the fulfillment of a dream.

It's so like God to provide even in our disobedience. Our job is to sit at His feet, worship Him and obey His directions. He gives the favor, increase and everything else we need. Daily, I am in awe of God and my heart is full of gratitude for the provisions He continues to make. We know the enemy doesn't give up that easily, so it is still a daily battle to trust and not fear because I must trust even on the days there are no orders and the bank account is low. Despite those circumstances, I trust Him and I declare Psalm 68:19, *'Blessed be the Lord, who daily loads us with benefits, The God of our salvation.*

Practical Application

What has caused you fear or anxiety lately? How did you respond?

_____
_____
_____
_____
_____
_____

How will you overcome the fear/anxiety?

_____
_____
_____
_____
_____
_____

Write a brief prayer to God about fear and anxiety – for where you are now or when it tries to creep in the future (because it will!).

_____
_____
_____
_____
_____
_____

Chapter 4

The Strange Place of Exhaustion

"When Gideon came to the Jordan, he and the three hundred men who were with him crossed over, exhausted but still in pursuit." (Judges 8:4 NKJV)

Exhausted. That's a very strong word. But, have you ever been there? The past few weeks have been extremely busy and today, I'm exhausted. It feels like I'm literally running on fumes. You know — one of those times when you're so tired that you can barely pay attention. I'm emotionally drained and a bit on edge because it *seems* as though *everything* is vital and due *all* at the same time. Church meeting, presentation to a potential client, gift basket orders to finish, a dentist appointment for mom who lives almost two hours away, unanswered emails and text messages. I am pouring through my calendar for a day to just stop, but there doesn't seem to be one for quite some time. I must find a moment because I'm *exhausted*. My current life's course caused me to recall a portion of scripture in Judges 8:4 NKJV, ...*exhausted but still in pursuit*. It is the story of Gideon and his army's pursuit against the Midianites.

Just two chapters earlier, in Judges 6, we can find Gideon hiding out and threshing wheat in a winepress. For seven years Israel has dealt with its neighbors, the Midianites and Amalekites, repeatedly raiding their land, destroying their crops and stealing their livestock. Weary of hiding out, they cry out to God for help – and He answers. God sends an Angel to Gideon who is hiding in a winepress threshing wheat, and the Angel greets him with the words, *'mighty man of valor.'* Wait, did we just read that a *mighty* man was *hiding*? That he's called *mighty* but is depicted as a man whose fear is greater than his faith?

Ok, let's talk. I can only imagine what you're thinking, but have *you* ever found yourself *hiding* during times of exhaustion? Let's examine this a bit more before you answer. You've been dealing with the same situation, same people, same illness, same child, same spouse, same bills for a minute now – and you're exhausted. You've tried to launch the ministry God placed in your spirit, but you can't seem to build the team you need. You've applied for promotion after promotion but have been turned down time and time again. You're overqualified or underqualified. You've tried three times now to get that home loan approved, but you've been denied…. again. You're exhausted and don't have the energy to try again. Your ego is bruised, but rather than being honest with God, you *hide* in insecurity, low self-esteem – and sometimes even arrogance. You hide behind a laundry list of excuses about why you are not pursuing what God has called you to, but the truth is – you're *exhausted*. I know. We are not supposed to be weary in well-doing, but in reality – we get tired.

> **We are not supposed to be weary in well-doing, but in reality – we get tired.**

When I'm extremely fatigued, my perspective is skewed. I don't think clearly and I'm more emotional. I'm also more likely to not feel my best physically. I've learned the hard way that rest is essential – especially now that I'm a *seasoned* citizen as my mother calls it. It is vital that we as believers understand the importance of caring for our temple so we can give God our best. That being said, let's talk about rest, and more specifically sleep deprivation, for a moment.

Believe it or not, sleep has become an evasive commodity for many. New data from *Sleep Cycle* has now shown that no country in the world manages to achieve eight hours of sleep on a regular basis. Additionally, the sleep achieved was not always considered *quality*. This highlights a troubling trend found throughout the world. Studies are replete with data about the impact the lack of sleep has on everyone – from young people to adults. We *need* rest to function properly. When we don't get it, we experience side effects such as irritability and a generally more negative mood; unhappiness and depression; low sex drive and lack of energy; problems with memory and retaining information, and weight gain with associated health issues. It is imperative that we rest so we are both physically and spiritually prepared for what life throws at us.

Like many of us, Gideon questioned God's presence with him given the situation he and Israel were in. *"If God is with us, why is all of this happening to us? Where are the miracles our ancestors told us about?"* Then he had a laundry list of reasons why he was not God's man for the job. *"My clan is the weakest in Manessah and I'm the runt of the litter."* Remember Israel in Numbers 13:33b when they were facing the giants in the Promised Land? *"Next to them we felt like grasshoppers, and that's what they thought, too."* Sounds familiar? We sometimes allow our circumstances to dictate how we see ourselves. It's an age-old tactic of the enemy that he's still using today. Daniel 7:25 warns us that he comes to, *'wear out the saints.'*

The enemy is subtle and strategic, and we can miss what he is doing. But, don't be ignorant of the things he is weaving into society *and the church*. We are often worn out and if you're like me, I miss key things when I'm tired. What are we missing as watchmen on the wall? What are we missing as parents and trusted adults watching over the lives of our children? What are we missing as spouses? We need to be on high alert –

> **Being well-rested is important to our ability to be on high alert to the tactics of the enemy.**

and being well-rested is important to our ability to do so.

But Gideon pivoted and so must we. Fast forward to Judges 8 and we will find the same man, Gideon, leading an army into battle after battle. They had been fighting for some time. In Judges 7:9 God told him, *"..Arise, go down against the camp, for I have delivered it into your hand."* Yet, in Judges 8, they are still fighting. Wait. What? God has *given* them the victory already, but they are still *pursuing* it? Yes! Here's a point to ponder.

Just like Gideon, you and I may have a promise from God that has not yet manifested. It's ours, but we must walk out the process to the manifestation. The process is often not pretty. Nor is it easy. We must be willing to press through the *middle*. To pursue despite the challenges. There *will* be challenges. And often, those challenges will bring us to a place of *exhaustion*. The closer we get to the victory, the more challenging the journey will become. You will feel like giving up. Get ready. Press. Push. Pursue. Now that we've been reminded about the enemy's strategy, we *must* prepare ourselves for the battle.

What battles are you facing right now? A hectic schedule - like me? As a stay-at-home mom, keeping up with the demands of caring for the children and the home? Being a good father and provider for your family? Final exams in college? Financial hardship? Health challenges? Broken relationships? You may be exhausted but stay in pursuit of all God has promised you. *'Go down and fight'* just as He commanded Gideon. Rest in the promise that victory belongs to you.

Here are a couple of important points to ponder. In Judges 8, Gideon asked help from some along the way. He shared that his army was exhausted and asked for *'bread,'* but was refused. I believe those people were protecting themselves from future backlash because they didn't have faith in Gideon's victory. Go ahead and prepare yourself now. There will be people who will not believe in your vision and they will not assist you when you ask for help. Oftentimes, it will come from those you least expect. Know that upfront so you are not dismayed when it occurs. Gideon didn't allow it to stop him. They pressed on despite the exhaustion, the lack of support, and the taunting. Trust God anyway.

Let's also not forget that the enemy will show up in your exhaustion *after* your victory. In I Kings 18, Elijah experienced great victory against the prophets of Baal. He'd seen the power of God in a miraculous way, but the threat from one evil woman sent him into a downward spiral. And what did he do? He went into hiding and into depression. Because we have a High Priest who understands us, God ministered to him as he rested. He allowed him to sleep and commanded a raven to feed him. Eventually, though, he had to get up from there and on to his assignment. God will give you a moment, but eventually your brook of comfort will dry up. We must get up from where we are and be about the Father's business.

I am a giver. I love helping people and I will give my last, not expecting anything in return. However, I've had to come to grips with the fact that those who receive the most are often the ones who give you the least – when *you* need. I've also had to learn that even givers must sometimes say 'no' in order give their best '*yes*' to the things they're called to. I'm not a pro at it yet, but 'I'm in pursuit.' They are what we call boundaries. Oftentimes as believers, we struggle with good boundaries because we worry too much about what people think. We don't want them to think we aren't 'good Christians.' Good boundaries, however, are *essential* to healthy relationships.

Let's talk boundaries for a moment. What is a boundary? Authors Henry Cloud and John Townsend in their book, *Boundaries: When to Say Yes, How to Say No to Take Control of Your Life*, defines a boundary as '*a property line*' that helps us distinguish our property so we can take care of it. In short, boundaries help us keep the good in and the bad out. They guard our treasures (Matthew 7:6) so that people don't steal them."

So often we are uncomfortable with setting boundaries, with telling people *no*. But Drs. Cloud and Townsend contend that setting boundaries helps us to have healthy relationships. Think about it. When we say no to things people are initially not happy about it. We can give in to their requests and be miserable, overwhelmed, frustrated, and angry as a result. Or, we can stand our ground. As time goes on, they are usually fine – and so are we. Sometimes we are exhausted because we've simply caved to other people's expectations and requests. I recall a situation in which an individual needed something when I wasn't available. Their response to me was *'we are available to God 24-7.'* Let's not even acknowledge the fact that they didn't provide what they were to provide which led us to that point. Normally, I would have done it and fumed about it, but I opted to respectfully acknowledge that I *was* (and still am) available to God 24-7, but not to them. That took courage and boldness, but I did it and it ultimately set the course for future encounters.

Many times, we sacrifice the *important* for the *urgent*. There are times when we place church *activity* above our families. I acknowledge that God has the place of pre-eminence in our lives and He should always be first. That doesn't mean, however, that all our activities get the same attention. I talked about seasons in an earlier chapter. Our priorities change with seasons. None of us are one-dimensional. We are believers, but we are also husbands, wives, mothers, daughters, sons, employees or business owners.

It is vital that we seek God and allow Him to guide us in being good stewards of each of those roles. I often talk about my current season and the fact that it is a new experience for me. First, I'm now a seasoned citizen with a few aches and pains of my own. And, I'm a daughter with two 80-something year old parents whose needs are very different now than they were in my earlier years. Just those two things alone have demanded a lifestyle change for me. I need more rest than before and when the parents call, I go. Nothing takes priority over their needs. Being a supportive, caring, patient daughter is a priority in this season. And, when I've completed my assignment for them, I need rest so I can function in the other areas of my life. As a result, I guard my schedule. Why? Because I left 2018 on the verge of exhaustion and all its cousins – frustration, depression, anger - and had to re-evaluate my life. I concluded that something had to go and as a result, made some lifestyle changes.

On that note, sometimes we are exhausted, but we will not relinquish control of some things to others and trust God to bless them as He did us. No, they will not do it the way you do. They are not you. And, truthfully, you had to grow to where you are, too. Find the right skill set (you can cultivate what is not there), train them and move on to the role of mentor/support. Allow them to develop what works for them and encourage them along the way. You can't go and stay at the same time. You'll create chaos.

> **Sometimes we are exhausted, but we will not relinquish control of some things to others and trust God to bless them as He did us.**

Then, there are those times when we will simply just not, *'be still and know.'* I'm guilty of this one. It's difficult for me to be still unless I'm asleep. I'm always thinking, researching, planning. But, I've had to learn to sit quietly and listen for the still, small voice of God – to recognize and obey it when I hear Him. Life is so much sweeter as a result. Do I still want all the answers now? Want everything in place so I know exactly how things are going to work? I sure do, but I'm learning to enjoy the peacefulness of resting in Him and ultimately being amazed at how He works things out for my good and His glory.

You're not there yet? No worries. Today's a great day to start over. Set the boundaries, release the exhaustion, pursue purpose and celebrate all that God has planned for your life. Your victory – and mine - is already *won*.

Practical Application

Think about a time when you were overly exhausted. What were the circumstances?

_____
_____
_____
_____
_____
_____

Map out a plan for reducing the amount of exhaustion in your life moving forward.

_____
_____
_____
_____
_____
_____

Write a brief prayer to God about setting good boundaries and your plan for reducing exhaustion so He gets your best yes.

_____
_____
_____
_____
_____
_____

Chapter 5

The Strange Place of Bitterness

"Don't call me Naomi," she responded. "Instead, call me Mara, for the Almighty has made life very bitter for me. I went away full, but the Lord has brought me home empty. Why call me Naomi when the Lord has caused me to suffer and the Almighty has sent such tragedy upon me?" Ruth 1:20-21 NLT

I can clearly recall one Wednesday night years ago my pastor was teaching from Ruth. In Chapter 1 verse 20 NLT, Naomi says something interesting as a result of her plight of having resided in a strange land and suffering the loss of both her husband and sons. She says, *"Don't call me Naomi. Instead, call me Mara, for the Almighty has made life very bitter for me."* Interestingly, while teaching he replaced Naomi's name with mine. He said, *"Don't call me Gwen. Call me Mara."* Now, it's not uncommon for preachers to do that at times, but his statement resonated with me in an unusual way. Did he just randomly choose *me* or was he implying that I'd allowed my circumstances to change me? And obviously not for the better? Looking retrospectively, it was the latter. I'd morphed into a totally different person – perhaps without even being fully cognizant of that fact.

In case you haven't grasped it, Mara means *'bitter.'* Like Naomi, which means *'pleasantness,'* I'd allowed the pain I was enduring to turn me a bit bitter and I certainly felt like someone other than myself. Interestingly,

Naomi made the declaration that she should be called bitter rather than pleasantness. It was her *choice*. So, how does one go from pleasantness to bitterness? What does that *transformation* look like? How does it happen? Let's start by defining bitterness and exploring its characteristics.

Bitterness is defined as *anger and disappointment at being treated unfairly; resentment*. According to *Psychology Today*, all bitterness starts out as hurt. Our emotional pain views whomever (or whatever) provoked the hurt (generally, our assumed '*perpetrator*') as having malicious intent: as committing a grave injustice toward us; as gratuitously wronging us and causing us grief. Anger—and its first cousin, resentment—is what we're all likely to experience whenever we conclude that another has seriously abused us. If left to *fester*, that righteous anger eventually becomes the corrosive ulcer we know as *bitterness*. It's why the Bible admonishes us to '*be angry but sin not*' and '*to not let the sun go down on our anger.*'

> **According to Psychology Today, all bitterness starts out as hurt.**

We are also admonished in Proverbs 4:23, to guard our hearts with all diligence because out of it flows the issues of life. Luke 17:1a ESV tells us, … '*Temptations to sin are sure to come.*' We can all be assured that there will be opportunities to become offended and hold on to the offense. But Genesis 4:7 NLT, tells us how to deal with it. It reads, '*You will be accepted if you do what is right. But if you refuse to do what is right, then watch out! Sin is crouching at the door, eager to control you. But you must subdue it and be its master.*' This is from the story about Cain and Abel, and we all know what happened. Cain killed his brother. It shows us firsthand what happens when we open ourselves to harboring anger and resentment. It brings other relatives, including *murder* potentially, with it. I hear you saying, '*I'd never kill anyone.*' Maybe not physically, but have you assassinated anyone's character? Have you killed anyone emotionally with your hateful, angry words? Ok, so you're not *that* bad. Has the *numbing* process started as a result of your bitter words and cold attitude?

Reality check. Bitterness does not happen overnight. It's a progressive process that we must handle immediately. We will all face the opportunity to be bitter but thank God, we don't have to seize it. So, let's talk about how to deal with it when it rears its ugly head. Let's start with prayer. I've learned how critically important it is to immediately pray when I am hurt and angry. There are many commands in scripture to do so. Colossians 3:8 tells us, *'But now you must rid yourselves of all such things as these, anger, rage, malice, slander, and filthy language from your lips.*' Ecclesiastes 7:9 reads, *'Do not be quickly provoked in your spirit, for anger resides in the lap of fools.'* Mark 11: 25 tells us, *'And when you stand praying, if you hold anything against anyone, forgive them, so that your Father in heaven may forgive you your sins.* Finally, Psalm 51:10 reads, *'Create in me a pure heart, O God, and renew a steadfast spirit within me.'* The speed of the results will depend on the situation. There are times when I can move on once I pray and the relationship is not impacted. Other times, I find that I need to have an open, honest conversation with the individual and once that happens, I can move on. Then, there are those times when the hurt is deep and/or recurring, and it takes much more to overcome it – including the possibility of severing the ties.

In all honesty, I have been deeply hurt and had a hard time letting it go. I tried but had to keep dealing with more and more hurt – which ultimately led to me feeling like I had a *right* to be angry and not forgive. That led to a root of bitterness. My whole demeanor changed because of the stuff in my heart. The truth is we can't hide the pain, the hurt for too long. There is a powerful quote that says, *'If you don't heal what hurt you, you'll bleed on people who didn't cut you.'* Ultimately something will happen that causes the poison to come gushing out onto someone – possibly those closest to us that we love the most. On the other side of it, I can now tell you that you don't have a right.

'If you don't heal what hurt you, you'll bleed on people who didn't cut you.'

The Bible tells us to forgive and that is what we must trust God's grace to give us the strength to do. It's for our good – and our growth. No, it doesn't let the other person off the hook. It gives God our permission to handle it on our behalf. And, it takes faith and a great deal of trust in a just God to do it. Jesus is our example. Not only did He forgive those who crucified Him, but He prayed for them. That's the key. When we can humble ourselves enough to pray for those who hurt and despitefully use us, it is then that God can get glory. So, you want Him to be glorified through your life? Get ready to die to your flesh! There will be many opportunities.

> **When we humble ourselves enough to pray for those who hurt and despitefully use us, God will get glory.**

The final point I will make about dealing with bitterness has to do with self-care. Many times, we overlook this important piece because we view it as being selfish. It's not. It's *vital*. When I was going through my divorce and went to counseling, the therapist taught me an acronym – H A L T. She advised that as I was going through this traumatic time, I should not allow myself to become too **h**ungry, **a**ngry, **l**onely and/or **t**ired. So often we do not pay close enough attention to our physical needs as we should. We think it's selfish, but I've learned the hard way that until I take proper care of me, I am not prepared to give my best to others. It seems so simple, but each of these four physical or emotional conditions represent basic needs that – when unmet - leave us vulnerable and susceptible to self-destructive behavior that can even include relapse for those battling addictions.

Now, I'm a Keyes by birth and we all know when one of us is hungry. My mother leads the charge. Lol! We're easily irritable so what wouldn't normally bother us, may very well do so when we're hungry. My energy level and my tolerance for things are at an all time low. It's also important to note that we shouldn't just look at these things on the surface so let's take a deeper dive.

Hunger can be a physical or *emotional* need. We all understand the need to eat, but we should strive to eat well-balanced nutritious meals. It helps our bodies to operate as they should. On the other hand, we may have a hunger for affection, accomplishment, encouragement, support and understanding.

Anger is a normal, healthy emotion if we handle it with care. Explore what is causing you to be angry and how to express it thoughtfully. You might even discover that you're angry at yourself. Deal with it quickly – whether that means talking with someone, exercising or even praying.

Loneliness can occur when we are alone or in a crowd. I've often been my *loneliest* in a crowd of people where I literally felt invisible. Can anyone relate? I've isolated myself when I felt that no one would understand where I was and what I was feeling; or when I felt fear and/or insecurity. That is the opportune time to pull on your support system and/or connect with others in a social setting.

Tiredness or fatigue takes a toll on our mind, body and spirit. I can now tell when it's coming on and no matter what others think, I know I *must* retreat and rest. Sometimes I need a weekend and at other times, just to stop and nap, listen to music, sit on my porch. Whatever you need, be sure you get it. Any one of these four can emerge as my response and I need to address them *immediately*. It is one of the reasons I guard my schedule and time the way I do. I know now where these things can potentially take me.

In our previous lesson, we discussed exhaustion and boundaries. I hope that you now see why it is so important to address both. Lack of healthy boundaries can lead to all four of these *and* exhaustion. We tend to just tire of everything when our emotions are out of whack. And, I now know that I am prone to walk down the path that ultimately leads to bitterness if these things go unchecked. We allow people to overstep our boundaries repeatedly, each time making us more and more tired of what we get as a result. If we fail to properly deal with it, bitterness will often become the result.

Now to the hard work of transformation. I remember flying high above the earth - looking through the clouds – during my flight to Memphis. I was broken and wounded – mourning and weeping internally while wanting to scream at the tip of my lungs. I was trying to process the pain so I could put on my *"I'm okay"* face by the time I reached my destination. And right there amid my struggle I heard the Holy Spirit say, *"There is purpose in your pain."* I had no clue what *purpose* the excruciating pain I could almost feel physically could play, but oddly enough I felt a sense of peace in that moment. I made it to my destination, fulfilled my assignment and moved on. But it wasn't over. It took prayer, a consistent diet of God's Word, and counseling to get me to a place of wholeness.

I had to recognize and acknowledge what I was harboring inside, get to a place of being sick and tired of being broken and bitter, then allow God to work on the broken places. I had to admit that my neediness and insecurity caused me to allow things that I shouldn't allow. I had to even acknowledge how some behaviors I exhibited was really *manipulation* and nothing was wrong with the person who wouldn't allow me to do it to them. It was hard then, but I appreciate them like crazy for standing firm on their boundaries. Admitting that my life was a mess was the first step toward my place of healing. Ok, God. You have my attention! Let's get to work.

Practical Application

Think about a time when you were either bitter or right on the cusp of being bitter. What were the circumstances? If you haven't dealt with it, please know that it may hurt and it won't be easy but do it now.

_____
_____
_____
_____
_____
_____
_____

Describe in detail how it both manifested and impacted your life?

_____
_____
_____
_____
_____
_____
_____

Write a heart-felt prayer to God about where you are and ask for His healing. Ask and allow God to break you in His Presence. Or, write a prayer of thanksgiving to God for your deliverance.

_____
_____
_____
_____
_____
_____
_____

Chapter 6

The Strange Place of Discipline

"For our earthly fathers disciplined us for a few years, doing the best they knew how. But God's discipline is always good for us, so that we might share in His holiness. No discipline is enjoyable while it is happening – it's painful! But afterward there will be a peaceful harvest of right living for those who are trained in this way." Hebrews 12:10-11 NLT

Have you ever witnessed a young child having a full-blown temper tantrum in public? I'm talking rolling in the floor, screaming, yelling at and talking back to the parent – all because they can't have the toy they want? And, this one grates my nerves at a level I simply cannot describe. It's a parent jerking the arm of and shouting profanity at a toddler because the child is essentially being a child! I bet that visual evokes all kind of emotions, doesn't it?

These scenarios are just examples of the kinds of chaos we see in our world today as a result of the lack of discipline. We read headlines like, 'Man threw hot coffee at McDonald's worker's face after waiting too long for fries,' and 'Pennsylvania man charged in *senseles*s and *savage* road rage killing after lane merge.' Ok, so you will probably never go to that extreme (although they probably never thought they would either), but do you think this just happened suddenly? Or, was it the result of an undisciplined life of allowing their emotions to go unchecked?

What is discipline and why do we need it? *Discipline* is defined as orderly or prescribed conduct or patterns of behavior; self-control; training that corrects, molds or perfects mental faculties or moral character. In the verb form, it means to train or develop by instruction and exercise, especially in self-control. Simply put, discipline is doing what we should even though we don't *feel* like it.

Like many of you, I don't *like* it either. However, I've come to realize that discipline is vital if there is to be any degree of greatness in my life. Does that mean I've mastered it? Not by any stretch of the imagination. In fact, I'm writing this as a result of looking at undisciplined areas of my own life – from my thought life to diet/exercise to some spiritual disciplines. I don't always immediately cast down negative thoughts when they come, sometimes I entertain them. I know I need to drink more water than I do. It will help my joints and my digestion. While I'm doing a lot better than I used to, there is still room for growth. I need more focus in my business pursuits and know I won't see the growth I desire until I do it. In fact, when one area gets out of sync, it tends to impact others. If I allow too many unscheduled interruptions, things like the time I set aside for prayer/study, exercise, and writing gets disrupted. It's so easy to do that I had to acknowledge it and ask God to help me.

> **Discipline is vital if there is to be any degree of greatness in our lives**

We didn't like it, but our parents knew the critical importance of instilling discipline early in our lives. How many of you can recall your mother saying things like, '*This is going to hurt me more than it hurts you*' – as she prepared to give you the whipping of your life with the switch or belt *you* had to bring to her? Do you remember being grounded for weeks while your friends were out having fun? My mother did not play when it came to discipline. She handled the business! I have some siblings who can testify to the fact that even if you tried to run – she would literally run you down. By the way,

I wasn't one of those she had to run down. She had a way with words that ripped my heart out.

I'm sure others of you can recall that the *village* could also discipline you. In other words, if you acted out in school, the teacher paddled you and by the time you got home, you had another one coming because your parents already knew what had occurred. And let's not forget that if the neighbor who lived down the street saw you acting out in the neighborhood, she would snatch you up, handle you and make sure your parents finished the job when you got home. No internet, no texts and certainly no cell phones, but news of your folly traveled like the speed of light. We didn't think so then, but in hindsight, those were the days.

We had structure and rules, and most of us obeyed them because we didn't want the consequences of not doing so. We had chores to complete. We had to make our beds daily and put our clothes away. We had to be in the house by a certain time and we couldn't talk on the phone after a certain time. We had to finish our homework before playing. We had to eat what was provided – including the vegetables – or we didn't eat at all. We couldn't just go in the fridge and get what we wanted. We had to ask, and we didn't always get what we requested. (My daughters still can't understand this). We had to put a handle on adults' names and show them respect even when they were mean and not respectful of us.

I didn't understand all the rules back then; however, now that I am older, I have great respect for them. They loved us and wanted us to be prepared when opportunities they could only dream of knocked on our door. Could some of it have been done differently? Absolutely! I believe with everything in me that they did their best. And after all, we turned out just fine.

Not long ago while at the nail salon, I had a very interesting encounter with a woman who identified herself as a therapist. She and her five-year old daughter agreed on the color nail polish the daughter could have before leaving home. However, her daughter was showing out in the salon because she wanted red – not the soft pink they had agreed to prior to leaving home. I looked on in amazement as she tried to reason with her daughter. I wanted so badly to handle it! Lol. As the mother and I had an opportunity to later converse, she shared that she was determined to rear her daughter differently than her parents had reared her. She went on to tell me that she just didn't feel that she needed to whip her daughter because she was *intelligent* and would respond to conversation and reasoning.

First, were *we* not intelligent? I'm here to tell you that her approach to dealing with her *intelligent* child was not working. I wanted to tell her that, but instead chose to ask questions that would hopefully help her face the uncomfortable truth staring her in the face. I asked, *'How is that working out?'* *'How many times do you have to speak with or negotiate with her?'* *'Does she respond with the kind of respect you gave your parents?'* *'What is wrong with the way you turned out?'* She really didn't have good answers. As one parent to another I simply reassured her that I understood her desire to be a better parent, but it was also vital to ensure that she was giving her child what she needed to be a successful, productive, and well-disciplined adult. She deserves that – especially in a society that seems to *look* for reasons to harshly discipline people of color.

When did discipline become such a bad thing? Please know that I am not an advocate of *any* form of abuse to children – or anyone for that matter. However, I am a huge advocate of appropriate discipline to ensure we are our best selves. I'm the mother of two adult daughters with whom I consider myself to now be great friends, but they still know that there is a line. I'm an old-school mom and I require respect just as I strive to give it. I care more about their well-being and character than about being friends with them. As children they had rules to guide activities and behavior. There were some things we could discuss, but others that were going to be what I decided – no discussion. Just as God, our loving Father, can see beyond what we see and guide us around things if we submit to His direction, we have the same role and responsibility as parents. It behooves us to exercise and not abdicate our God-given responsibility in this critical hour.

The Bible is replete with scriptures about the importance of discipline. Hebrews 12:11 NLT tells us, 'No discipline is enjoyable while it is happening – it's painful! But afterward there will be a peaceful harvest of right living for those who are trained in this way.' Proverbs 13:24 NLT says, 'Those who spare the rod of discipline hate their children. Those who love their children care enough to discipline them.' Loving discipline shows us that there are consequences to our actions and that we must be accountable. The ultimate goal is to lead us to Christ and discipline is a key part of the process.

> **Loving discipline shows us that there are consequences to our actions and that we must be accountable.**

Discipline is a *strange* place. It's uncomfortable because it goes against the grain of our natural inclination. Apostle Paul writes in I Corinthians 9:27 NLT, *'I discipline my body like an athlete, training it to do what it should. Otherwise, I fear that after preaching to others I myself might be disqualified.'* I Thessalonians 5:17 NLT tells us, *'Never stop praying.'* II Corinthians 10:5 MSG reads, *'We use our powerful God-tools for smashing warped philosophies, tearing down barriers erected against the truth of God, fitting every loose thought and emotion and impulse into the structure of life shaped by Christ.'* In I Corinthians 6:18 NLT, we are told to *'Run from sexual sin! No other sin so clearly affects the body as this one does. For sexual immorality is a sin against your own body.'* In Matthew 5:44 NLT we are told, 'But I say, love your enemies! Pray for those who persecute you!' Mark 11:25 NLT tell us, *'But when you are praying, first forgive anyone you are holding a grudge against, so that your Father in heaven will forgive your sins, too.'* Then Psalm 27:14 MSG tells us, *'Stay with God! Take heart. Don't quit. I'll say it again: Stay with God.'* These, and other scriptures, are designed to help us become disciplined in our walk with the Lord. They cover so many areas that do not come naturally for us, so we can't do them on our own. We must die to our flesh and surrender to the Spirit of God daily. And yes, it takes discipline and commitment to do so. It is not optional if we're to walk into the fullness of the opportunities and assignments God has for us. If we stay with God and follow the process, we will begin to see a life that honors and brings glory to God. I am always so in awe of God and how He orchestrates my life.

Heretofore, I've focused on discipline from an individual perspective, but here's an eyeopener as it relates to leadership. While writing this chapter, I *happened* to be reading a devotional entitled, The Discipline of Planning. It's an amazing devotional that essentially highlights the meticulous planning Nehemiah did to ensure success in rebuilding the wall of Jerusalem. He began with prayer then planned, and God gave him favor. As I read it, I began to assess my business goals and plans, and had to admit to myself and to God that I was *'weighed in the balance and found wanting,'* (Daniel 5:27 NLT). In all honesty, I was a bit discouraged that I wasn't seeing the business results I wanted, but the study let me see that I wasn't as disciplined in my planning and execution as *I* needed to be.

The point that really hit home was a story in day five of the devotional about two explorers – Roald Amundsen and Robert Falcon Scott – each of whom, in 1911, set out to be the first in history to reach the South Pole. Long story short, Amundsen was very disciplined in planning every detail of the trip. Scott, on the other hand, planned haphazardly. He didn't discipline himself to properly plan for challenges, including weather. As a result, he reached the South Pole *one month after* Admundsen and his team *left*. Even worse, his entire team died on the way back – because of his lack of discipline and commitment to proper planning and preparation.

It hit me like a ton of bricks! As a leader I have a responsibility to properly plan and oversee the vision I'm asking people to share in with me. I must develop the discipline to drench the vision in prayer, to be crystal clear about what God is leading me to do and identify the appropriate people and resources to get the job done. At the end of the day, the lives of those

I'm asking to join me depends on it. Has someone's passion for ministry, a cause, their assignment *died* because of your lack of discipline? Let that marinate for a moment.

What areas do you need to work on? Exercising and eating right so you can stop taking medicine or avoid surgery. Maybe it's in praying and reading your Bible daily. It might just be that you need to better manage your time. Or your finances. Your use of social media. Controlling your emotions. Being more diligent in planning and executing the vision as a leader. Oh, wait – maybe it's in the area of *waiting*. I challenge you to look deeply and identify your area(s), then ask the Father to help you conquer them.

> **Has someone's passion for a cause, their assignment, or even ministry died because of your lack of discipline?**

So, how do we go from being undisciplined to living a disciplined life? Here are a few tips. Begin with a consistent diet of prayer and the Word. Then, make a commitment to doing something productive *every* day. Focus is critical – so set hourly and daily goals and stay focused on them. Refocus as needed. Think about and adjust your daily routine as necessary. Create a plan or a list of the things you want to get done and do it. Finally, get a mentor or an accountability partner. As *strange* or uncomfortable as discipline may seem, don't be a stranger to it. You'll need it at every stage of your life, and I promise you won't regret making the sacrifice.

Practical Application

Identify an area of your life where you either need discipline or a greater level of discipline. Identify the reason you need to be more disciplined.

_____
_____
_____
_____
_____

Develop a 21-day plan to address the need. Be sure to include daily declarations/affirmations from the Word of God. (It takes 21 days to create a habit)

_____
_____
_____
_____
_____
_____
_____

Write a heart-felt prayer to God about the area you identified asking God to help you develop the discipline you need. Be sure to thank Him for your deliverance.

_____
_____
_____
_____
_____
_____
_____

Chapter 7

"But they that wait upon the Lord shall renew their strength; they shall mount up with wings as eagles; they shall run, and not be weary; and they shall walk, and not faint."
Isaiah 40:31

Have you ever been inspired by the Word and your faith was ignited to the point that you just knew that you were next? In fact, you believed in your heart of hearts that your blessing wasn't coming not next – but *now*. A month passed and you were yet holding strong, trusting God to come through. Now, a year, two years, ten years, 25 years have passed, and you are yet *waiting*.

Raise your hand if you *love* waiting. I wish I could see who, if anyone, raised their hands. I can assure you that I would probably not be one of them. Why? Because waiting is *hard*. Whether you're waiting for the traffic light to change, the microwave to finish heating your food, at the hospital or doctor's office, or for the arrival of a beautiful, sweet newborn – waiting is difficult.

Waiting is also inconvenient. After all, we're busy people who must get things done so we can move on to our next big thing. Waiting also means delayed gratification in a society where we are accustomed to getting what we want - quick, fast and in a hurry. But guess what? God is rarely in a hurry because He is not bound by time. In fact, the Bible tells us in 2 Peter 3:8 NLT that, '...*A day is like a thousand years to the Lord, and a thousand years is like a day.*' So, while waiting may be a *strange* and quite uncomfortable place for us, it is a place that God often calls us to occupy. *Strange,* but it is a sure and safe place when we're seeking to be in the perfect will and timing of God. That's why the enemy uses the tactic of impatience to lure us out of the place of safety and onto his path of destruction.

> **The enemy uses the tactic of impatience to lure us out of the place of safety and onto his path of destruction.**

Even when we *do* wait, many of us do not wait *well*. Why? It takes great discipline to do so and as we discussed in our previous lesson, many of us live undisciplined daily lives. We huff and puff, groan and complain, and often work half-heartedly. Waiting well requires us to believe God against the odds, no matter the situations we may face. It requires us to draw nigh to God through a constant diet of prayer, the Word, worship and encouragement from strong believers.

> **Even when we do wait, many of us do not wait well.**

When we don't wait well, we produce fleshly efforts to help God out. Here's a perfect example. God promised Abram and Sarai a son, but they waited so long that He changed their names during the wait as a reminder that He had not forgotten His promise. But waiting was hard for them just as it is for many of us. So, they devised a fleshly plan and sent Sarai's handmaiden, Hagar, to Abram and they produced a son. Notice that it was a *son* just as God had promised, but he was not the *child of promise*. He was a counterfeit and their actions led to all sorts of problems. Sounds familiar? It didn't matter how long they'd waited or old they were, God still had the power to produce what He promised. However, it would only come in His timing, without any assistance from them. As a matter of fact, He waited until they were so old that it was humanly and naturally impossible. That's the God we serve. He lets us come to the end of ourselves so everyone knows it wouldn't have happened as it did except God was with us. When we wait and allow God to fulfill the promise, He will get *all* the glory. My friend, it doesn't matter how long you've been waiting on your promise, you can be assured that He has not forgotten you.

I prefer not to wait a long time, but in my heart of hearts I want to be in the will of God. I want to obey Him. The spiritually mature part of me really wants to *'wait patiently on the Lord,'* but if I'm honest, my flesh wants it now! For me – and probably most of you - I believe therein lies the problem. The battle rages between our spirit and our flesh *even* in the wait. Psalm 31:15 tells us that our *times are in God's hand* and if there is one thing I'm sure of; it's that God's timing is perfect – but vastly different than ours.

Despite our disdain for it, waiting on the Lord has many benefits. Waiting helps to develop our character. Oftentimes in the wait, God shows us who we *really* are and the things in us that must be crucified. When true character is developed, we will see things through to the end no matter how long a commitment it requires, with no pat on the back, and purely for God's glory. In the wait, we find out if our motives are pure or if we are just trying to garner attention for ourselves.

Waiting also helps us develop patience. Our fast-paced society has taught us great impatience even in small things. We get upset when someone is going too slowly in the passing lane and we border on a bit of road rage. We will almost throw a conniption fit if we wait too long for our *fast* food. Even our little ones become impatient if we take too long responding to their needs. Patience is a fruit of the Spirit (Galatians 5:22) that must be developed in the life of every believer. James 1:3-4 reminds us that, *'The testing of our faith produces patience, and when our patience is fully developed, we will be mature and complete, needing nothing.'*

While we are waiting, we learn to trust God implicitly as He guides us through the process of becoming more like Him. It's in the wait that we are given instructions that lead us to new levels in our relationship with God. He may work on a spirit of unforgiveness and replace it with love; or He may lead us through the process of getting bitterness out of our hearts. Sometimes, He teaches us to be quiet and not speak everything that comes to our mind so we can handle the places where He will ultimately allow us to operate – whether in ministry or the marketplace.

As we yield control and begin to rest in Him our trust grows. When we trust Him, we will embrace His unconditional love, His discipline, His instruction and direction – and we will see growth and development as a result. Think about it. Do we give our children a car before they are mature enough and have been trained to drive it? Do we give thousands of dollars to a toddler? Absolutely not! In the same way our loving Heavenly Father makes us wait for many of the blessings He has for us until we are mature enough to properly handle them. And, the maturity comes through the wait.

Waiting should also inspire a sense of anticipation. Think about the excitement we feel when it's approaching our birthday and we want to see what goodies we'll receive. Or when someone tells us they have something for us. We should have that kind of anticipation or expectation about what is on the other side of us waiting on God. He has already assured us that our strength will be renewed, and we will soar like the eagle. It's in the wait that He gives us what we need to soar, to excel, and to be all He has called and created us to be.

In the wait, we must be watchful and cognizant of the enemy's devices because while waiting has many benefits, there is also the potential to become discouraged and question God's love for us. We see this in St. John 11 in the story of Mary and Martha when their brother Lazarus died. Because of their special relationship, they expected Jesus to come quickly.

When He didn't and Lazarus died, they were disheartened because they believed things would be different had Jesus been there. How many times have you said, or thought, that God would come to your rescue quickly because of your relationship with Him? And, how did you feel when He left you waiting right there in the situation? Frustrated? Discouraged? Like He didn't care? Like giving up? The truth is, He does care. He cares enough not to leave us where we are. In the wait, God teaches us to relinquish control and surrender our will completely to Him. I am becoming so much more keenly aware of just how much we want to be in control, to know all the details.

I've also found that waiting can bring about extreme loneliness and what may even feel like rejection. To get us where we need to be God will sometimes isolate us. During a time of fasting and prayer, we may be cut off from everyone - even on social media. At other times we may see all that others are doing via their social media posts while God has us in a holding pattern with no one to even check on you. I remember a point in time feeling

> **To get us where we need to be God will sometimes isolate us.**

like, '*God, where are all the people I supported in their time of need?*' His reply was simply, '*Don't you think I know where you are and what you need?*' My tears were my humble response back to Him.

Being still and waiting on God is an extremely *strange* place for me because I'm a doer. It's difficult for me to sit still unless I'm asleep. As a result, I've sometimes missed precious moments with Him. I can only imagine the intimacy I would have experienced if only I'd taken my focus off the *wait* and put it on worshipping. I probably would have finished this project sooner for when there is true intimacy, we give birth – to our promise, our dreams, to new ministries, to businesses, and to books.

Let me encourage you today, God cares about you (and me) so much so that He sent His Son to die for us. He loves us beyond our imagination, so hang in there. Get busy serving while you wait. Ultimately, we'll come to find out that it was well worth the *wait* when we experience the *weight* of His Glory resting on us.

Practical Application

What is something you've been waiting on for a while, but still haven't received.

Share your honest thoughts are how you have been waiting.

Write a heart-felt prayer to God about what you have written and memorize two scriptures about waiting.

Chapter 8

The Strange Place Conflict and Confrontation

'So if you are standing before the altar in the Temple, offering a sacrifice to God, and suddenly remember that a friend has something against you, 24 leave your sacrifice there beside the altar and go and apologize and be reconciled to him, and then come and offer your sacrifice to God.' Matthew 5:23-24 TLB

Conflict. Confrontation. What emotions do these words evoke? For many of us, perhaps fear. I would venture to say that conflict and confrontation probably rank in the top five things we either fear or dread. Ecclesiastes 1:9 reminds us that there is nothing new under the sun, however. Conflict has been around for ages and we even see examples in scripture. In Genesis 13, Abraham and Lot went their separate ways because of conflict among their shepherds. Remember Paul and Barnabas? Acts 15 records the conflict between them concerning John Mark that ultimately led to their separation. And, of course, we've all probably heard about Euodia and Syntyche, the two women in Philippians 2:2-3, whom Paul asked his co-laborer in the Gospel to help resolve their conflict. I can think of a lot more biblical instances of conflicts as I'm sure you can, too.

Let's get on the same playing field relative to what conflict is. It is defined as *a serious disagreement and argument about something important*. As such we often view conflict negatively. However, given my background in human behavior and conflict management, I want to delve a little deeper. In conflict management theory, conflict is defined as *different objectives and attitudes between two or more parties*. Simply put, parties in a conflict often have different needs, goals, or desires, but perceive that if one gets what he/she wants the other will lose. They see only a win-lose option, but an often-overlooked fact about conflict is that it is neither good nor bad. It is how we choose to deal, or not deal, with conflict that shifts the outcome, quality of relationships, the culture and life in general. A great example from college is about two chefs who both needed the one lemon that is available. Imagine the conflict when both their recipes in the competition needs a lemon. Effective communication, however, allowed them to see that they could both get what they needed from the *one* lemon. After the first chef squeezed the juice, the other was able to use the peel for his lemon zest. Simple. I know, but a profound example of how a little communication can often help resolve what appears to be a big issue – especially in stressful situations.

> **How we choose to deal, or not deal, with conflict is what will shift the outcome, quality of relationships or the culture.**

Confrontation is defined as *a hostile or argumentative meeting or situation between opposing parties*, and as a result is also often viewed negatively. In conflict management theory, however, confrontation is key to the healthy resolution of conflict. It is defined as *the direct expression of one's view (thoughts and feelings) of the conflict situation and an invitation for the other party to express his/her views of the conflict*. Confrontation allows each party to describe the behavior of concern and his/her reaction to that behavior. Can you sense the difference just from the definitions?

Conflict is inevitable in any type of relationship involving individuals because we are all unique and we each bring different perspectives to the table. But we can garner greatness from the diversity in our unique perspectives *if* we handle them with openness and respect. Of course, this is what the enemy does not want to happen because of the Kingdom impact it will have. We have allowed unresolved conflict to run rampant for far too long. Even our families, homes, workplaces, our world, and even some of our faith communities are fraught with conflict. Racial tension and hatred fill our news headlines in 2019! Nevertheless, it's time for us to wake up, build our capacity to confront conflict, and live in love and unity as we are commanded to do. Our relationships, families, churches, organizations, and our world will be better as a result. I know. It's not easy. I didn't say it would be. As a matter of fact, for many of us it is a *strange* and very uncomfortable place to even think about. We tell ourselves it's better to just let it go, but if we're honest we'll admit that we stew in it – sometimes to the point that it turns into bitterness. You know how it goes. There is something that happens inside of us at the very sight of that individual. I've been there and done that!

Now don't get me wrong. I don't address every situation because it's not reasonable. But I have a rule that I generally follow. If I can process the situation and move on without it impacting my behavior and how I treat the person, I do. If it eats at me and I can't move on, I address it with the individual if they will allow it. I aim to do that before it becomes a major problem. I can own what I'm feeling by saying something like, '*When X happened, it made me feel Y.*' Or by asking, '*Is something wrong? I seem to sense that there is something going on and I wanted to check in about it.*' In doing so, I haven't *accused* anyone and therefore, have hopefully not put them on the defensive. I've simply stated how the action or behavior made *me* feel and opened the door for more conversation. Yes, it puts you in a bit of a place of vulnerability, but that will likely be the case with any relationship we value.

Reconciling our differences is vital for us as believers. Jesus prayed in John 17:21 NLT, 'that we would be one as He and the Father are one.' He also told us in John 13:35 NLT, 'Your love for one another will prove to the world that you are my disciples.' When conflict arises, we must follow the mandates of the Word in order to have the quality relationships God desires for us. Though we often fail to confront issues, scripture provides us a prescription for doing so. Let's look at some Biblical guidelines for addressing conflict. Matthew 18:15 MSG tells us, 'If a fellow believer hurts you, go and tell him—work it out between the two of you. If he listens, you've made a friend. If he won't listen, take one or two others along so that the presence of witnesses will keep things honest, and try again. If he still won't listen, tell the church. If he won't listen to the church, you'll have to start over from scratch, confront him with the need for repentance, and offer again God's forgiving love." While this speaks specifically to a situation within the church, clearly we can glean principles from it that we can use at home, work or elsewhere. This is simply mediation or assistance in resolving a conflict.

> *Reconciling differences is vital for believers.*

James 1 addresses conflict from a more global perspective. In verses 1-2 MSG we read, 'Where do you think all these appalling wars and quarrels come from? Do you think they just happen? Think again. They come about because you want your own way, and fight for it deep inside yourselves. You lust for what you don't have and are willing to kill to get it. You want what isn't yours and will risk violence to get your hands on it.' This speaks to the earlier point about parties seeking only their needs without any thought about how the other parties will be affected. It also made me think about the headlines concerning the current president's racist tweets that are dominating the news currently. It is a classic example of one having *no* regard for how his comments affect those who are not in agreement with him, yet they are among those whom he is elected to serve.

There are so many more scriptures I could share, but let's look at one final passage that I believe is critical. We use a lot of excuses for not confronting, but I want to challenge you to do your part in helping to manage conflict in your sphere of the world. Matthew 5: 23-24 TLB tells us, 'So if you are standing before the altar in the Temple, offering a sacrifice to God, and suddenly remember that a friend has something against you, leave your sacrifice there beside the altar and go and apologize and be reconciled to him, and then come and offer your sacrifice to God.'

Imagine for a moment that you're in Old Testament times. You've traveled from home to the Temple, purchased your animal sacrifice, and are presenting it to the priest when suddenly you remember that a neighbor or family member has something *against you*. God, you want me to do what? Leave my gift, go work it out and come back? But, can't I do this while I'm here *then* go handle the situation – since I'm not the one with the issue anyway? By the way, have you noticed that obeying God is often not convenient? I certainly have. So, what's *really* the deal here? It's about serving God with a clear conscience. About dealing with anything that has potentially gone wrong in our relationships – as much as lies within *our* power.

There should be no question in our minds about how God feels about the quality of our relationships. In John 13:34-35 TLB He tells us, 'And so I am giving a new commandment to you now—love each other just as much as I love you. Your strong love for each other will prove to the world that you are my disciples.' With so much happening in our world today, the need for our witness is greater than ever. Our light must shine even brighter in the boundless darkness that exists. With that in mind, I want to interject a concept from a recent devotional I read titled, *Caring Enough to Confront* by David Augsburger. He talks about the importance of care when we confront, and as a result coins the word, *carefronting*. It isn't often that we find these two words together, but it's the Biblical way.

Carefronting is offering genuine care that lifts, supports and encourages. It is being upfront with important facts that can call out new awareness, insight and understanding. It is loving and level conversation that unites the love one has for the other with the honesty and truth we can see about each of us. It allows us to be genuinely loving without giving away one's power to think, choose, and act because in such honesty, one can love powerfully *and* be powerfully loving at the same time. 'Carefronting,' he says, '*is the most valuable secret for reforming conflicts. To be truly for the other person even as you stand for what you value is not just to be adept at interpersonal communication. It is to be adult.*'

> **'Carefronting is the most valuable secret for reforming conflicts. To be truly for the other person even as you stand for what you value is not just to be adept at interpersonal communication. It is to be adult.'**

For far too long, we have made excuses for not confronting conflict as we've been instructed in God's Word. The time to repent and do our first works is now. Let's not get comfortable in the *strange* place of *unresolved* conflict. Conflict is inevitable, but let's try a little carefronting.

Finally, so what happens when we've exhausted our efforts to resolve conflict, but to no avail? The Bible addresses that also. It tells us in Romans 12:18 NLT, 'Do all that you can to live in peace with everyone.' The reality is that there will be some relationships that simply cannot be saved. You are only required of God to forgive and to do what *you* can to resolve the issue. If the other party/parties refuse to do so, there is nothing you can do but pray. Do that and move on. I know. In some cases that will be easier to do than in others. Know how to keep outside people *outside*. And, allow God to heal you from the pain of hurt from those *close* to you so you can enjoy the abundant life He has planned for you. I've had to walk this one out and I can tell you it takes a great deal of humility. You *must* crucify your flesh, but it is well worth the sacrifice. I've not only seen what can happen, I have experienced this firsthand. While it was difficult initially, God has truly brought me to a place of peace and for that I am most grateful.

Practical Application

Think about a conflict situation you are/were involved in. How did you handle it? What, if anything, could/should you have done differently?

_____
_____
_____
_____
_____
_____

Implement the concept of carefronting in a current situation, one you need to go back and address or when conflict arises. Describe the results.

_____
_____
_____
_____
_____
_____

Write a heart-felt prayer to God asking His help in handing conflict and confrontation in loving/caring way.

_____
_____
_____
_____
_____
_____

Chapter 9

The Strange Place of Singleness

'Two people are better than one, for they can help each other succeed.' Ecclesiastes 4:9 NLT

I recently had the opportunity to watch a video of an interview conducted with four successful African American women. It was so impactful that it gave birth to this chapter. While it highlights huge implications for African American women, I saw even broader implications for women in general that I had not thought in depth about heretofore.

The video shed light on what I call singleness and how it disproportionately affects African American women. Some of you reading this may be like me, in that I am not sure if I'm interested in being anything other than single – most days that is. Nevertheless, there are many of my sisters who *want* to be in a relationship or married. For many of them, though, singleness is a *strange* and sometimes disheartening place. The more I pondered the information in the video, it appeared to me that there is something even deeper to be considered and that, my friends, is what I *really* want to talk about. So, let's jump in.

Data from the YouTube video titled *3-6 Million US Black Women Can't Find a Husband or Boyfriend*, is startling. Now, it's no surprise to me that there are more women than men but hearing that there are approximately 1.8

million *more* women was staggering. The situation is further exacerbated by the number of men with no high school diploma, no job and who are incarcerated. In fact, the data reported that 42% of black women, double that of our white counterparts, have *never* been married – a phenomenon referred to as the '*black girl curse.*' That then led to questions like, '*Do we settle or compromise?*' '*Do we date outside our race?*' As a matter of fact, data shared in the video stated that the rate of African American women entering interracial relationships has more than doubled in the last decade.

The women also spoke about the '*Friday girls*' – those with whom men hook up just for sex and the, '*back pocket girls,*' those women who are '*on hold*' by eligible men who check in periodically to see if the ladies are still single – hoping they will be available when they are *ready* to settle down. 'Are our standards too high or are the pickings too slim?' are just a couple of questions some women are asking. The picture is bleak for those women who desire to be in relationship with a strong black man.

But black women have always been strong – *right?* In fact, I came from a long line of strong women. They did what they had to do. Worked and performed miracles with the little money they made, reared the children, took care of the home, helped their neighbors and supported the church. They did all of this, oftentimes neglecting themselves. They were our examples, our sheroes and for many years we followed suit. We worked, cooked, cleaned, served and gave our best to our families, church and community – and we should invest time in these things. Even on Mother's Day, we – the ones being celebrated – in many instances did the cooking and serving.

Recently, however, I led a revolution in my family. I realized that I was tired. Still strong, but tired. And not ashamed to admit it. After all, I'm single. I have some business ventures I'm working to grow. I help to provide the care and support my parents need as they are aging. I have a home, a car, and my own life to manage and, I assist my church administratively. Funny story - now, but not when it was happening. I had a week recently when several things happened back to back. I discovered that because I enter my home through the garage and rarely use my front door, some birds had helped themselves to an area right above the door. They built a nest which I discovered as a result of seeing a small egg on the porch while retrieving a delivery. Because there were tiny little birds in the nest, we couldn't remove it until they could fly. Day in and day out, I had to endure the chirping and clean up their mess. It was utterly disgusting, and I was totally embarrassed for even the delivery man to come to my front door. And the mother bird had the nerve to be territorial – as if she owned something! They almost attacked my neighbor who brought some mail that was put into her box accidentally.

About the same time, my sliding glass door off the kitchen suddenly stopped working leaving my home unsecured until I could find a reliable repairman. Then, the batteries to the fire alarms in my 8-foot ceilings that I can't reach needed to be changed. One would chime 'low battery' and the other would echo the same message – *day and night*. As if that wasn't enough while working at the kitchen table one afternoon, I noticed something in the grass coming up from the pond. For the first time in my three years in the house, I saw a snake in my yard. By this time, I was ready to put my retirement home on the market. In all seriousness, the *last* thing I wanted *that* week was to deal with anyone else's issues, problems or requests. I was done. It was a very stressful week as I tried unsuccessfully to get all those issues addressed.

Here is where it gets broader. There are many singles in the world today – among our families and friends, in our workplaces, and certainly our places of worship. Some are single as in never married, single again after divorce, single parents – *single*. There are many benefits to singleness, but as I thought about that week, I realized that there are also challenges. It is during times like those that I feel the *weight* of singleness, of having to handle *everything* alone. I find that those are also the very times I often get calls or texts about what others – family, business, church - need. And it is during those times when I sometimes don't *feel* strong – when I want to just sit and cry my heart out. It is in those moments that I come to grips with the fact that I don't have a strong shoulder to cry on or someone to simply say, 'No worries. I've got you. I'll take care of that. Just relax.' I must add what has suddenly come up to what I handle routinely. For those of you saying, 'You've got Jesus,' so very true. But in this moment, I'm speaking now of a *physical* presence. And by the way, you have Him too – *and* a partner.

> **While there are many benefits to singleness, there are also the challenges of handling everything alone.**

Whether in our family, our church, or among our friends, there *seems* to be this notion that single people have an inordinate amount of availability. After all, we're *single*. What do we have to do – right? We may not have the same responsibilities as married couples but remember that we also don't have the *support* from another individual like couples do. We do it all – *alone* – most, if not all, of the time.

This is a faith-based book, so let's talk scripture. I know we emphasize from I Corinthians 7:32-35 that singles have a greater degree of freedom that positions them to work for God without concern for the responsibilities of caring for a family – and the Bible is right. However, we can't forget that singles also have lives with issues, challenges and the demands of *single* life. In fact, we must also consider that there are single women (and men) with children. As a single, now seasoned woman, I want to raise awareness about what I would consider the unrealistic expectations that singles sometimes face. Here's why.

There is more and more data about depression and the importance of checking on those who are *strong*. About the 'Superwoman Syndrome,' a term coined by clinical psychologist, Jazz Keyes (no we're not related – that I know of). Simply stated, it is the burden of strength passed down through generations, lessons handed down from grandmother to mother then mother to daughter. It is the belief that we can do it all on our own, have it all, and be all things to all people *all* the time. It is prevalent in the women who take care of everyone else. The ones who take a licking in life, but keep it moving. The ones we can always depend on. The ones we ask for help because after all, they are single and have extra time and resources to spare – so we think. Because of this mindset; however, it is said that many African American women suffer from a sense of inadequacy - not because they aren't successful, but because they aren't *'successful enough.'* That mindset can then lead to stress, anxiety and a series of mental health issues like depression.

I can tell you stories for days about a time in my own life when I put my needs on the back burner because someone else *needed* me. Of course, we are not to be self-centered but I'm here to tell you that you can't pour from an empty cup – no matter who you are – woman or man, African American or otherwise. That self-care is not *selfish* at all. It is necessary. It is imperative that you know when to pull away and allow God to lead you beside still water so your soul can be restored. I've learned

> **For too long, we have been strong for everyone else while sometimes battling our own emotional traumas in silence.**

the hard way that I am not superwoman nor anyone's savior. I have learned to stand my ground when I say that I can't take on something, regardless to what others may think, say or feel. For too long we have been *strong* for everyone else while sometimes battling our own emotional traumas in silence.

As I am writing this, my mind took a mental flight to a time when I worked on a project that I ultimately couldn't even enjoy when it happened because I was sick. I'd worked so hard and so much without proper rest and nutrition, that I ended up sick. It wasn't anyone else's fault. I'd pushed past the signals *my* body gave because I was in the zone. I loved what I was doing. That's fine, but we must learn how to listen to our bodies and share the load with others by delegating. I could park there, but that's another whole book.

More recently, I attended a training that was about strategies for business building, but the facilitator first led us through an exercise designed to help us look at ourselves. She gave specific instructions about what to do, but I was a bit distracted and had unknowingly not followed instructions. When she noticed that I had moved on to page two, she kindly asked why. She then used it as an example to show us how we as women often take on more than we need to at times, putting pressure on ourselves. As she talked, tears began to stream down my face despite my *best* efforts to hold them back. She was describing *exactly* where I was at the time. It was one of those times when life was happening in an 'all at one time way.' I was trying to juggle it all because I strive to be a woman of my word, but I needed to take a step back and readjust.

It was a bit embarrassing to sit amidst my sisters and cry. Why? It initially made me *feel* weak. She was so smooth in the way she handled it, however, that I gained an appreciation for it despite the discomfort I felt. She didn't acknowledge my tears, she simply kept doing what she was there to do – yet I *felt* her compassion. I could also see the concern on the faces of the small intimate group of my sister entrepreneurs in the room – that simply said it was a *safe* space to be vulnerable. That's a lesson in itself – but perhaps for my next book. Though they said nothing verbally, I knew they understood and supported me. It was an experience I will not soon forget, and it has helped me on my journey to better self-care as I serve others.

I speak for many strong, single African American women (and other women, too) who are like I was for a long time - reluctant to assert their voice. We love God, our families, you and what we do for you – but sometimes we *just* need a break. We may not want to get into all the details about why. We want you to trust and respect our decision. While writing this book and for the second year in a row, I was called back for a follow-up after my annual mammogram. Of course, I prayed and trusted God, but it was also a somewhat stressful time – a time when I needed to focus on me and my health. I am most grateful that it's all fine – simply a small benign tumor that requires no further action. Now that the tests are behind me, I can perhaps focus on someone else and what they may need – but in that moment was simply not the time.

Let's go a little deeper. When was the last time you asked a single woman, or man, how he/she was doing – *really*? Not to help you, borrow money, babysit, work extra hours, or serve an area of ministry, but simply 'how are you *really* doing?' Have you said, 'You're often here for me. How can I assist you?' Have you given any thought to how some may feel lonely – and may *be* alone much of the time given that so many people now live miles away from their families? How many may be grappling with depression? Or illness? Or struggling to break toxic relationships? Do you ever wonder what it feels like for them to go home to an empty bed *every* night while you snuggle with your beloved?

Here is another challenge specifically for ministries. Women and men are single much longer now than in years past – if they marry at all. This begs the question of what ministries can do to help singles – both younger and older - navigate the *strange* place of singleness. The dangers of singleness for those who want love and marriage. Of helping singles maintain the lifestyle of purity we preach in our highly sexualized culture. Ever thought about how often singles are excluded from sermons except for when the subject is about sex? Or how many times we hear, '*Why are you still single? You're so beautiful.*' Or, '*Just stay faithful. God is going to send the right one when you're ready.*' That implies that there just *might* be something wrong with us or that we have more work to do before we're ready for marriage. That may be true in some cases, but there are also married people who have things to work on.

The Bible admonishes us to embrace our singleness – whether for a season or a lifetime. But with that came the promise of a family within the church – children, brothers, sisters, mothers, and God as our Father – along with the promise of eternal life according to Mark 10: 29-30 NLT. Perhaps it is time that we rethink ministry to singles and what it should look like in this era.

I am so incredibly blessed to have an amazing support system – from my daughters to my parents and siblings. I'm determined to enjoy life and live it to the fullest. I travel. I create. I read. I find opportunities to be involved with others. I work my small businesses. My life is full, yet I have *moments* of loneliness. I have moments of wondering what it will be like to grow older *alone*. To support myself without the benefit of someone to share the load. I think about how I will manage if I were to get sick. I know we are not to 'worry, but instead pray about everything' according to Philippians 4:6. Yet, these are real concerns for me as I'm sure it is for other singles. Sure, I have family, but this isn't *solely* about me. I have friends and colleagues who are single and have lost much of their family. Some who never married or had children.

Like me, some of them are committed to ministry and to serving in the community. Some are caretakers of their parents, siblings, and even aunts and uncles who have been blessed to live longer lives. Some are even caring for others as they are aging and, in some instances, also ailing. It is a great blessing – and a *strange* place all at the same time. And, it requires some rest and support that we perhaps didn't need earlier in life. We need more than to just be an answer to ministry needs. We need to know we are loved. And, we need discipling and shepherding – with an understanding of our *unique* circumstances. We need deposits and not just withdrawals, so we don't live bankrupt lives. And a brief perusal of articles showed me that this isn't only true for African American women – but other ethnicities as well.

I know that married people have their own unique set of challenges, but this chapter is about the *strange* place of singleness – with all the joys and challenges thereof. Much of what is talked about is couples-oriented, so this chapter gives a 'singles' perspective. Singles with lives, responsibilities, struggles, and challenges just like you. We acknowledge that what you deal with may be magnified given that you have a family, but please do not minimize what we are experiencing because we fly solo. The bottom line is that we are all part of a great big family – some married and some single. Just like our natural families, we all have needs.

The scripture says, 'Two is better than one, for they can help each other succeed.' A young single person may not need the support of a peer in the season he/she is in, as they may be dealing with some of the same challenges. He/She may need *you* – seasoned man or woman of wisdom – to provide guidance, support and love that his/her peers cannot possibly provide. I've heard some ask, 'Where are the mothers? Fathers? Who will pour into us?' On the other hand, some of you, young singles, must understand that God wants to accelerate your maturity so He can serve *you* up to your generation. Give Him a *yes*. It will require you to say *no* to some things you really want to say *yes* to but make the sacrifice.

I know we're all busy, but perhaps it's time to re-evaluate our priorities, clean up our schedules and avail ourselves to the souls calling out for help. Like any other *strange* place, God also meets us in our singleness. It is one of the reasons we must ensure we don't over-extend ourselves and crowd out our time with Him. He is the God of all comfort. He bids us to come pour out our hearts to Him. We can share every care, fear and concern. We can cry and tell Him our deepest secrets and rest assured that we won't hear them again. He promised us that if we would acknowledge Him in all our ways, He would direct our path.

Single lady (and man), let God help you. Remember the horrible week I talked about earlier? He sent me help. My amazing neighbor brought in his ladder and changed all the batteries, and the only pay he would accept from me was ginger ale – which he loves. My angel of a handy man took care of my door and a few other issues. When I paid him, he tried to give some of it back. Instead we agreed that he'd come back, remove the bird's nest and power wash my house once the birds could fly.

We must face the challenges of singleness, but we have an ever-present God who will help us when we call. Two of my all-time favorite scriptures are Jeremiah 33:3 MSG, 'Call to me and I will answer you. I'll tell you marvelous and wondrous things that you could never figure out on your own' and Isaiah 65:24 NLT, 'I will answer them before they even call to me. While they are still talking about their needs, I will go ahead and answer their prayers. What precious promises. Sure, we have some challenges but don't be discouraged. Embrace and enjoy your single days, trusting God to fulfill every need in your life. I promise you – He will if you'll embrace His will and trust His process.

> *We must face the challenges of singleness, but we have an ever-present God who will help us when we call.*

Practical Application

Write out at least one AHA moment from this chapter.

_____
_____
_____
_____
_____
_____

What can you do to address it/make a difference?

_____
_____
_____
_____
_____
_____

Write a prayer to God asking His help in carrying out what you can do to help.

_____
_____
_____
_____
_____
_____

Chapter 10

The Strange Place of Peace

Don't worry about anything; instead, pray about everything. Tell God what you need, and thank Him for all He Has done. Then you will experience God's peace, which exceeds anything we can understand. His peace will guard your hearts and minds as you live in Christ Jesus. Philippians 4:6-7 NLT

As I come to the close of the book, I am amazed at the place in which I now find myself. I can sense that I am in a very different place than when I began as though writing has somehow brought me healing, freedom – and peace. What's interesting is that some of my circumstances have not changed. But, I have. Make no mistake. I have not arrived, but I've certainly moved from where I was. That's progress.

I'm sure there have been times of challenge and chaos in your life just as there have been in mine. Times when life happened and rocked your world. The reality is that we'll have more of them. The Bible tells us in Job 14:1 ESV, 'Man who is born of a woman is few of days and full of trouble.' In other words, life is short and will not be full of just good times. We *will* experience times of challenge so we might as well brace ourselves for it. Does that mean it will not hurt or feel uncomfortable? That it won't catch us off guard or feel *strange*? Not a chance.

James 1: 2-4 MSG reads, 'Consider it a sheer gift, friends, when tests and challenges come at you from all sides. You know that under pressure, your faith-life is forced into the open and shows its true colors. So, don't try to get out of anything prematurely. Let it do its work, so you become mature and well-developed, not deficient in any way.' Yes, you read that correctly. We are to consider the tests and challenges we experience in this life a *gift* that helps us to essentially grow up in God. To develop our spiritual muscles. To grow in wisdom that positions us to minister to others. Now we all know that is easier said than done. Please understand that it's a process that we must submit to daily – sometimes hourly or even minute-by-minute. Philippians 4:6-7 has instructed that the way to keep our peace in those situations is by talking to God about *everything* – not just the big things, but everything. God is concerned about everything that concerns us so He invites us to come pour out our hearts to Him in prayer or conversation, and thank Him for all He's already done. When we do, we will experience His peace.

So, what distinguishes the peace world gives from the peace that Jesus gives? Worldly peace is basically a state of harmony, quiet and/or calm. Think about it as a still pond without ripples. However, that alone doesn't see us through tragedy and persecution. It's why we see people, even among the wealthy, who end their lives under the pressure of trouble. But Jesus gives us something much deeper. He was so committed to our peace that while He was on His way to the cross, He stopped to leave us a parting gift. He promised in John 14:27 TLB, 'I am leaving you with a gift—peace of mind and heart! And the peace I give isn't fragile like the peace the world gives. So don't be troubled or afraid.' In other words, Jesus offers us the same help - *a transforming, inner work and source of power by the Holy Spirit* - that He had in facing the cross.

> **Jesus offers us the same help - a transforming, inner work and source of power by the Holy Spirit - that He had in facing the cross.**

We experience that inner work as *peace* when facing our own hardships and suffering.

The walk of faith is so very *strange* and goes against the grain of our natural inclinations. Think about it. Who in the world rejoices *in* tough times and pain? I'm not talking about once we're out, but *in* it. It's what we are called to in the Word. True peace requires faith in God and His Word. It requires us to shift our focus off our circumstances and onto our great God. Our world is greatly troubled. My heart has been grieved and full of compassion for the families that have suffered senseless tragedy this past week – shootings, stabbings, and the disappearance of children. I simply cannot fathom the pain they are feeling. I don't have a direct relationship to any of them but know the pain I feel for them. I was encouraged, though, as I watched one family declare their faith and trust in God despite the tragic loss of their daughter and granddaughter who yet remains missing. They epitomized the saying, 'peace is not the absence of trouble. It is the presence of Christ *in* of our trouble.' That is what it means to experience true peace. And yes, it may both look and feel *strange* to have what seems like the world crumbling around you – yet you are at peace.

Here is something else to keep in mind. There will be those who'll misunderstand that level of peace. I've seen instances where people didn't understand someone else's response to death because the individual(s) didn't grieve like them. Equally so, there will be those who may not understand your response of peace right in the center of chaos, confusion and pain. As I think about this my mind immediately goes to Mark 4:35-41, the account of Jesus asleep on the boat in the middle of a raging storm. As water began to fill the boat, the disciples panicked and awakened Him – asking if He didn't care that they were about to be overtaken by the storm and drowned by the waves. Calmly, Jesus simply spoke to the winds and waves saying, 'Peace, be still' then spoke to the disciples about their lack of faith.

I've had to endure tumultuous winds of trouble and waves of adversity in my life. And like the disciples, in all honesty, there were times when I panicked, too. While 2019 began as a year of panic, it has morphed into a year of me *intentionally* seeking God diligently for the strength to trust Him *no matter what*. Of me constantly reminding myself that He is a loving Father and it is His good pleasure to provide for me. A year of me clinging to the promises of His Word – that reminded me just yesterday from Psalm 46:5 that, 'God is within me, and I cannot fail.' It's been a year of me learning to speak *'peace'* to my storms. You and I must never forget that we have the power to *'speak'* peace to the situations in our lives. It is an act of faith that must be lived out daily. I've come to realize how powerful daily affirmations are – especially those that come from the Word of God. When things begin to go awry (and they will) and I feel a bit anxious, if I will stop right then and focus on the Word and worship the atmosphere shifts. That act affirms that I serve a mighty God who is in control no matter what the situation looks like – and that I trust Him more than what I see. Anyone can believe and trust when things are good, but it takes faith to trust and remain in peace when life's storms are raging all around us.

> **Anyone can believe and trust when things are good, but it takes faith to trust and remain in peace when life's storms are raging all around us.**

A month or so ago, I had the privilege of speaking to our congregation from the subject, 'You're in Labor and It's Time to PUSH.' The main points were essentially words that began with the letter P -Pray, Press, Persevere and Praise. The U was for Until, S was Shift and H was Happens. We must do all these things to keep our peace amidst trials. Just this week I was reminded of the fact that must sometimes fight to keep our peace. It will just not come easy.

I can very vividly remember the day I realized that I'd finally shifted into the *strange* place of peace after my divorce. One of the things that helped me tremendously was taking a hot bath nightly. I *had* to have hot water and soothing aromas like lavender to help me sleep. Then one day, after about three months, I realized that my routine was changing. Shortly thereafter, I read an article about how hot baths helped to eliminate toxins from the body. God was shifting me, and I didn't even realize it. I had many issues to deal with, but He gave me peace of mind – and the clarity I needed to make sound decisions. He brought me to the point that I finally acknowledged that I couldn't control my circumstances. Once I laid them at His feet, I found the *strange* place of peace.

The hymn, 'What a Friend We Have in Jesus,' reminds us that we often forfeit peace because we don't carry *everything* to God in prayer. The peace of God is so important in our current age. The world is full of anxiety. Even our children live with a heightened sense of anxiety as a result of things like school shootings, safety drills for potential active shooter incidents, and missing children reports. We must keep a watchful eye even when we go to worship nowadays. In all of this, God still calls us to the place of peace. Initially, it will feel a bit *strange* not to carry the weight and pressure we sometimes become accustomed to carrying. But it won't take long for us to embrace and enjoy the sacred space of peace. It is the place God is daily leading us to – the place of complete trust and dependence on Him. The place of peace that transcends even our own understanding.

How do we get there? Isaiah 26:3 NLT tells us, 'You will keep in perfect peace all who trust in you, all whose thoughts are fixed on you!' When our thoughts wander, we must bring them back in line. We must speak the Word of God over our thoughts and emotions – no matter how we feel and how *strange* it may feel in that moment. As we do,

> **We must speak the Word of God over our thoughts and emotions – no matter how strange it may feel in that moment.**

we will sense God's peace. He can use our testimonies of victory, of experiencing His peace amidst chaos to do as He did – impact the world.

Personal Reflection

What have you not had peace about lately?

_____
_____
_____
_____
_____
_____

What is one thing you can do today to move you towards the place of peace concerning the situation?

_____
_____
_____
_____
_____
_____

Write a prayer to God asking His help in finding His peace concerning the situation.

_____
_____
_____
_____
_____
_____

Bonus

The Strange Place of Repentance

If you openly declare that Jesus is Lord and believe in your heart that God raised him from the dead, you will be saved. 10 For it is by believing in your heart that you are made right with God, and it is by openly declaring your faith that you are saved.
Romans 10:9-10 NLT

Perhaps reading this book has caused you to realize that you have some changing to do. That's the awesome thing about God – He is gracious. When we come to ourselves, as the prodigal son did, we can always come home to the Father. He is so glad to welcome us home that the feast begins the moment He sees us approaching '*home.*' The return is easy. He only requires that we come – not cleaned up and put together – but just as we are. All that matters is that His blood was shed for us on Calvary many years ago.

He's been waiting so if you're ready, today is your day to get a fresh start. Whether you're a believer who hasn't come to fully trust Him and has forfeited your peace, or you're someone who's never opened your heart and invited Jesus in – today I invite you to the *strange place of repentance*. It is so simple that many find it difficult to believe and embrace. They struggle to *receive* His Grace – but it's as simple as the ABC's.

A - Admit

Admit to God that you are a sinner. Repent, turning away from your sin.

"For all have sinned, and come short of the glory of God." Romans 3:23

B - Believe

Believe that Jesus is God's Son and accept God's gift of forgiveness from sin.

"While we were sinners, Christ died for us." Romans 5:8

C – Confess

Confess your faith in Jesus Christ as your Savior and Lord.

"If you will confess with your mouth, "Jesus is Lord," and believe in your heart that God raised Him from the dead, you will be saved." Romans 10:9

Now, if you'll pray this prayer with me, salvation and all it brings with it *will* be yours today.

Dear God,

I am sorry for my sins. I believe Jesus died on the cross for my sins. Please forgive me. I ask Jesus to come into my life to be my Savior and Lord. Thank You for loving me and saving me from my sins.

In Jesus Name, Amen

If you prayed that prayer, you are now a member of the family of God. This is just the beginning of a wonderful new life in Christ. To deepen your relationship, you should:

1. Read your Bible every day to know Christ better.
2. Talk to God in prayer every day.
3. Tell others about Christ.
4. Worship, fellowship, and serve with other Christians in a church where Jesus Christ is   preached.
5. As Christ's representative in a needy world, demonstrate your new life by your love and concern for others.

No matter what you've heard or once believed – leave it all behind and embrace your new life in Jesus Christ. He loves you more than life – and I do, too. Welcome to the family of believers!

Afterword

It has been an absolute joy reading this book. I believe the author, Gwen, has given practical yet profound principles on how to navigate through *"strange places."* So many people are going through difficult times and need to know that they are not alone. Not only are they not alone, but we serve a God who is close to those in distress and discomfort. It is in those times that, no matter what we may feel, God is closer than we think.

It has always fascinated me that God volunteered Job for tribulation. He said to Satan, "*Have you considered my servant, Job?*" I need you to understand that though you have been or may be in a strange place, you have been considered. In other words, God trusts you with trouble. He trusts that in transition you will hold on to Him. We often talk about how we trust God, but what an incredible feeling to know that God trusts us!

On a personal level, I happen to be the older daughter of the author and can personally attest to the fact that she has been in some *"strange places."* There were times when I could literally see how trouble began to change her. I saw the lack of confidence. I saw the hurt and pain. I saw the struggles - both emotional and financial. I saw the strong woman I once knew begin to fade away. I have seen her give and give and never receive from those she sacrificed so much for. I have seen her push other people's dreams and vision at the expense of her own.

But, she has grown and overcome to the point that I know God is saying, "Now, I know." It is because of this that she is more than qualified and equipped to pen such an amazing work of literature. It is *strange places* that have made this special person, Gwendolyn Keyes Baker, and I am so proud to be her daughter!

Kristen D. Baker

Minister, Worship Leader, Author

Works Cited and References

Retrieved from http://www.bibleanswerstand.org/discipline.htm

#creator, & #identity. (2013, July 30). From Pleasant To Bitter. Retrieved from https://www.sermoncentral.com/sermons/from-pleasant-to-bitter-chuck-sligh-sermon-on-bitterness-177848

1. Retrieved from https://www.bible.com/reading-plans/11185-caring-enough-to-confront-by-david-augsburger/day/1

10 Reasons to Embrace the Season of Life You're In. (n.d.). Retrieved from https://www.google.com/amp/s/www.crosswalk.com/faith/spiritual-life/10-reasons-to-embrace-the-season-of-life-you-re-in.html?amp=18 unexpected - and negative - things that could happen when you lose weight. Retrieved from https://www.google.com/amp/s/amp.insider.com/negative-side-effects-of-weight-loss-2018-1

Altrogge, S., Altrogge, S., Reyes, L., Emmanuel, Mark, Wendt, R. D., … Athena Baron. (2018, November 5). 4 Life Changing Ways To Wait On The Lord (and 3 Huge Blessings). Retrieved from https://theblazingcenter.com/2018/03/wait-on-the-lord.html

(2018, June 1). Avoiding Assumptions and Caring for Christian Singles in the Church. Retrieved from https://radical.net/articles/avoiding-assumptions-and-caring-for-christian-singles-in-the-church/

Bauman, J. (2019, February 25). HALT: The Dangers of Hunger, Anger, Loneliness, and Tiredness. Retrieved from https://bradfordhealth.com/halt-hunger-anger-loneliness-tiredness/

Cloud, H., & Townsend, J. S. (2017). *Boundaries: when to say yes, how to say no to take control of your life*. Grand Rapids, MI: Zondervan.

Conflict Among Believers. Retrieved from https://billygraham.org/story/conflict-among-believers/

(2008, February 1). Conflict Resolution. Retrieved from https://www.focusonthefamily.com/lifechallenges/relationship-challenges/conflict-resolution/a-biblical-guide-to-resolving-conflict

(2014, March 16). Elements of a Living Sacrifice. Retrieved from https://www.gty.org/library/sermons-library/80-414/elements-of-a-living-sacrifice

Horan, L. (2016, September 15). This Data Shows A Shocking Worldwide Lack of Sleep. Retrieved from https://www.dreams.co.uk/sleep-matters-club/data-shows-a-shocking-worldwide-lack-of-sleep/

Lawless, C. (2019, July 25). God's Mission Has an Enemy: 10 Facts about Spiritual Warfare. Retrieved from https://www.imb.org/2017/05/17/mission-enemy-10-facts-spiritual-warfare/

Misael, Randy, Palmer, A. A., Bamigboye, J., Makubung, A., & Guthrie, R. (2017, April 4). What It Means to Believe With the Heart (Part 1) – Kenneth E. Hagin. Retrieved from https://www.hopefaithprayer.com/faith/kenneth-hagin-faith-lesson-no-8-what-it-means-to-believe-with-the-heart-part-1/

Prayer, Y. D. (2017, November 21). A Prayer for When You Don't Know What to Do - Your Daily Prayer - June 1. Retrieved from https://www.crosswalk.com/devotionals/your-daily-prayer/a-prayer-for-when-you-don-t-know-what-to-do-your-daily-prayer-november-24-2017.html?utm_source=Your Daily Prayer&utm_campaign=Your Daily Prayer 20Crosswalk.com&utm_medium=email&utm_828775&bcid=d436bc665adca459ab511a3208353632&recip=546889911

Prayer, Y. D. (2017, January 10). A Prayer to Wait on God without Losing Faith - Your Daily Prayer - June 6. Retrieved from https://www.crosswalk.com/devotionals/your-daily-prayer/a-prayer-to-wait-on-god-without-losing-faith-your-daily-prayer-january-11-2017.

html?utm_source=Your Daily Prayer&utm_campaign=Your Daily Prayer - Crosswalk.com&utm_medium=email&utm_

833655&bcid=d436bc665adca459ab511a3208353632&recip=546889911

Prayer, Y. D. (2017, April 18). A Prayer for Fear and Anxiety - Your Daily Prayer - July 18. Retrieved from https://www.crosswalk.com/devotionals/your-daily-prayer/a-prayer-for-fear-and-anxiety-your-daily-prayer-april-20-2017.html?utm_source=Your Daily Prayer&utm_campaign=Your Daily Prayer - Crosswalk.com&utm_medium=email&utm_

875718&bcid=d436bc665adca459ab511a3208353632&recip=546889911

Richard, C. (2018, April 5). 6 Spiritual Seasons of Life (and How to Flourish in Them). Retrieved from https://www.ibelieve.com/faith/6-spiritual-seasons-of-life-and-how-to-flourish-in-them.html

Seasons of Life. Retrieved from https://www.google.com/amp/s/leewoof.org/2014/09/23/seasons-of-life/amp/

(2019, August 20). Single, Satisfied, and Sent: Mission for the Not-Yet-Married. Retrieved from https://www.desiringgod.org/articles/single-satisfied-and-sent

Taylor, M., Keife, B., Rihtarchik, B., Dance, R., Riggs, D., Paschall, A., ... Sandra. (2016, September 6). When You're Waiting on God in a Lonely Season. Retrieved from https://www.incourage.me/2016/09/waiting-on-god.html

The Discipline of Planning. Retrieved from https://www.bible.com/reading-plans/14406-the-discipline-of-planning

The Story: Bitterness. Retrieved from https://www.google.com/amp/s/jasonbybee.com/2013/04/17/the-story-bitterness/amp/

Three Reasons Why Every Woman Should Embrace Fear. Retrieved from https://www.richdad.com/resources/rich-dad-financial-education-blog/february-2016/three-reasons-why-every-woman-should-embrace-fear

Two Are Better Than One: The Blessing of Marriage - Resources/Articles ‹ Congdon Ave. church of Christ. Retrieved from https://www.knowthelord.org/resources/2011/12/01/two-are-better-than-one-the-blessing-of-marriage

Undisciplined Life. Retrieved from https://www.google.com/amp/s/arshidferoz.wordpress.com/2017/03/20/undisciplined-life/amp/

What Does "Wait on the Lord" Mean? How to Be More Confident in Waiting. Retrieved from https://www.biblestudytools.com/bible-study/topical-studies/how-do-we-wait-upon-the-lord.html?utm_source=today's+topical+bible+study&utm_campaign=today's+topical+bible+study+-+biblestudytools.com&utm_medium=email&utm_

55056&bcid=d436bc665adca459ab511a3208353632&recip=546889911+

(2018, August 29). When the Generation Gap Comes to Church. Retrieved from https://www.crcna.org/spe/resources/spe-published-items/when-generation-gap-comes-church

Why Did Jesus Sleep During the Storm? Retrieved from https://www.google.com/amp/s/www.thegospelcoalition.org/article/jesus-sleep-storm/?amp

Woods, J. (2018, May 26). The Black Superwoman Syndrome, Busy-ness, and Depression. Retrieved from https://www.withoutaspace.com/shared-space/2018/5/26/the-black-superwoman-syndrome-busy-ness-and-depression

Your Pride Is Not the Only Problem - Topical Studies. Retrieved from https://www.biblestudytools.com/bible-study/topical-studies/your-pride-is-not-the-only-problem.html?utm_source=today's+topical+bible+study&utm_campaign=today's+topical+bible+study+-+biblestudytools.com&utm_medium=email&utm_43796&bcid=d436bc665adca459ab511a3208353632&recip=546889911+

Zoschak, G. Why Do Believers Fear? Retrieved from https://www.cfaith.com/index.php/blog/23-articles/victory/19421-why-do-believers-fear

About the Author

Gwendolyn Keyes Baker is a mother of two amazing daughters, a ministry leader, entrepreneur and author with a wealth of wisdom to share. Her career spans almost 30 years in state government and the nonprofit sector. In February 2019, she retired to fully pursue her long-time passion of entrepreneurship.

Currently an Independent Consultant with Mary Kay, Gwen is taking a 'more than skin deep' approach in her personal development workshop series called TreasureTalks - designed to help women discover the hidden treasure within. She is also a Paparazzi Accessories Consultant and owner of Simply Elegant Gifts.

Gwen has written her first book which is scheduled for release in September 2019. She is co-owner of MD Publications, a Christian Publishing Company through which her book is published.

She has an undergraduate degree in Social Welfare from SC State University and a Master of Arts in Human Behavior and Conflict Management from Columbia College.

Gwen has a passion for serving women and seizes every opportunity to positively impact lives.

For bookings:

Visit www.gwendolynkbaker.com to book Gwendolyn Keyes Baker for speaking engagements or to book a TreasureTalk to Go on *Finding God in Strange Places*.

If you have questions or need additional information, please call us at 803-386-7398.

Contact Us:

MD Publications

Irmo, SC 29063

803-386-7398

www.mdpubs.world

www.ingramcontent.com/pod-product-compliance
Lightning Source LLC
Chambersburg PA
CBHW020234170426
43201CB00007B/423